YOUR BUSINESS YOUR PENSION

If you want to know how...

The Management Speaker's Handbook
*Templates, ideas and sample material that will transform
every speaking occasion*

Patrick Forsyth

This unique book presents concise and practical advice on content and technique, and provides specific guidance in the form of blueprints for over 25 individual speaking situations.

How to Make Your Point in Just a Minute
*Get to the heart of the matter quickly and make your listeners
want to hear more*

Phillip Khan-Panni

'I have heard Phillip speak on this subject many times and every time I learn something new. Now his book gives me all those good ideas in a format that I can dip into over and over again.'

howtobooks
Send for a free copy of the latest catalogue to:
How To Books
3 Newtec Place, Magdalen Road,
Oxford OX4 1RE, United Kingdom
email: info@howtobooks.co.uk
http://www.howtobooks.co.uk

YOUR BUSINESS YOUR PENSION

How to use
your business
to provide for
**A BETTER
RETIREMENT**

JOHN WHITELEY

howtobooks

Published by How To Books Ltd,
3 Newtec Place, Magdalen Road,
Oxford, OX4 1RE, United Kingdom.
Tel: (01865) 793806. Fax: (01865) 248780.
email: info@howtobooks.co.uk
http://www.howtobooks.co.uk

First edition 2005

British Library Cataloguing in Publication Data
A catalogue record for this book is available from
the British Library.

Produced for How To Books by Deer Park Productions, Tavistock
Typeset by *specialist* publishing services ltd, Milton Keynes
Printed and bound by Cromwell Press, Trowbridge, Wiltshire

Note: The material contained in this book is set out in good
faith for general guidance and no liability can be accepted
for loss or expense incurred as a result of relying in particular
circumstances on statements made in the book. The laws and
regulations are complex and liable to change, and readers should
check the current position with the relevant authorities before
making personal arrangements.

Contents

Preface

Providing for your retirement has never been so urgent a topic as it is now. At the time of writing this book, there has barely been a week go by without some item in the newspapers relating to pensions in some form or another. Yet most people are turned off by the subject.

I hope that this book will serve as a wake-up call to those who are tempted to put off providing for their retirement. Although it is specifically aimed at people running small businesses, the methods of contributing to your pension can be used by anybody. I have tried to set out the possibilities in plain, non-technical language. Inevitably, however, certain technical terms are used. I have tried to explain these, and there is a glossary of terms at the end of the book. There is also, following this preface, a list of the abbreviations used in writing about pensions. Put a bookmark in that page so that you can refer to it when you come across the abbreviations.

Throughout this book there are tips to help you make provision for your retirement in the most tax-effective way. Look for them highlighted in boxes in the text.

I place on record my thanks to the people who have helped me compile this book. First, my publisher who suggested this book, and encouraged me to write it. Certain technical information has been supplied by the James Hay Pensions

Consultancy. Ian Avery, the pensions consultant of City Wall Financial Management Ltd. has been more than generous with his time in reviewing the content and suggesting areas that needed to be covered. Last, but by no means least, thanks to my wife, who has put up with my obsessions while writing this book.

John Whiteley

List of Abbreviations used

I have tried to keep technical jargon to a minimum, and explain the subject in plain English. However, a certain number of abbreviations are unavoidable in this subject, and the list below explains what they mean. Keep a bookmark in this page to refer to it when you come across one of these abbreviations.

APP   Appropriate Personal Pension

APT   Association of Pensioneer Trustees

AVC   Additional Voluntary Contributions

CETV   Cash Equivalent Transfer Value

COFSS   Contracted Out Final Salary Scheme

COIPS   Contracted Out Individual Pension Scheme

COMPS   Contracted Out Money Purchase Scheme

EPP   Executive Pension Plan

FSAVC   Free Standing Additional Voluntary Contributions

FURBS   Funded Unapproved Retirement Benefit Scheme

GMP   Guaranteed Minimum Pension

IPA   Individual Pension Account

ISA   Individual Savings Account

LPI   Limited Price Indexation

MFRC   Minimum Funding Requirement Certificate

NRS   Notional Reference Scheme

OMO   Open Market Option

OPRA   Occupational Pensions Regulatory Authority

PPP   Personal Pension Plan

PT   Pensioneer Trustee

RAP   Retirement Annuity Policy

RPI   Retail Price Index

S2P   State Second Pension

SERPS   State Earnings Related Pension Scheme

SIPP   Self Invested Personal Pension

SSAS   Small Self Administered Scheme

UURBS   Unfunded Unapproved Retirement Benefit Scheme

1
Introduction

Providing for your retirement

You may only just have started being self employed, or running your own business. So when do you start to think about retirement? The answer is – now!

It is never too early to start providing for your retirement. Any delay severely reduces the final benefit when you retire. Self employed people pay class 2 and class 4 National Insurance contributions. Class 2 contributions only qualify you for the basic State Pension, and *class 4 contributions do not qualify you for any pension at all*. They are simply an extra tax on the self employed. Anyone who has tried to live on the basic State Pension will tell you that it is not enough.

The importance of pension planning

When you are in business, your energies are directed towards making a success of the business – and rightly so. You are in business because you believe you have a good service or product, and you believe that you have the ability to deliver that product or service to the people who need it, thereby making yourself a living.

But you should be focusing at least some of your energies on providing for yourself after you retire.

- Perhaps you want to pass the business on to your family.
- Perhaps your aspiration is to retire early – maybe in your fifties, or even in your forties.
- Perhaps you really don't see yourself as stopping and doing nothing, so you want to continue some kind of gainful activity even into your later years.
- Perhaps you don't see yourself as retiring at all, and you want to carry on until you drop.

Whatever your aspirations, you must do something to provide the means to be able to enjoy those years in some comfort – or at least without having to bear unnecessary financial worries. And even if you imagine yourself in that category of carrying on until you drop – think of your dependants. Spare them the worry and despair of having to cope in difficult financial circumstances.

The message is quite clear – you must think about, and do something about providing for your retirement. More than that – you need to do it now! Whatever stage you are at in your career, it is never too early to start saving for your retirement.

The urgency of pension planning

The pensions crisis

The State Pension system in this country is not on a 'funded' basis. That means that when you start paying National Insurance contributions, they do *not* go into a fund to provide for a pension for your retirement. They go on providing pensions for people who are presently retired. This causes its own problems in an ageing population.

As our life expectancy increases, the average age of the population increases – this is known as an ageing population. So, the more people over retirement age, the greater the amount of pensions which have to be provided by people who are still working and paying National Insurance.

> **Example**
> If 10% of the population is drawing a pension, those pensions are being provided by the other 90% who are working and paying National Insurance. In other words, it takes nine working people to supply one retired person's pension. As the average age of the population grows, so fewer people are paying for more people's pensions. So, if 20% of the population is drawing a pension, the other 80% are paying for them. This means that there are now only four working people to pay for each retired person's pension. And as the average age increases, this problem gets even more acute.

Here are the actual figures – currently, there are 27 pensioners for every 100 people of working age. By 2050, there will be 48 pensioners for every 100 people of working age.

In response to this growing problem, the government is encouraging people by tax incentives to make more provision for their own pensions, either privately or through employers' schemes. There are moves to extend the retirement age, or at least to encourage people to put off drawing their State Pension for longer.

The political dimension

The political importance of this topic was seen in November 2004, when high court judges threatened to leave their posts because of the proposed lifetime cap on pension contributions attracting tax relief (see Appendix 1). The government hurriedly put through a bill to exempt judges from this restriction.

The danger of putting it off

Consider the case of twin brothers. They start work on the same day, when they are 20 years old. The wise brother starts saving immediately £100 per month into his retirement fund. Assuming a steady interest rate of 5% on his savings, by the time he is 65, he will have a retirement fund of nearly £203,500.

The foolish brother puts off saving for his retirement. If he puts it off for five years, his retirement fund will be only just over £153,200 by the time he is 65. If he puts it off for 10 years, his retirement fund by the age of 65 will only be just over £114,000.

Put it another way – if the foolish brother puts it off for five years, he will have to save £132.80 per month to get the same retirement fund as his brother. If he puts it off 10 years, he will have to save £178.37 per month to get the same fund. And the figures get progressively worse for each extra year he puts off saving for his retirement.

Uncomfortable facts

Consider these statistics:

- The Prudential estimates that two million pensioners are in financial difficulty. The average annual income for retired households in the U.K. is £14,648. The average drop in income at retirement is £4,164. 2.8 million pensioners are returning to work to meet this shortfall.

- One in seven people entering retirement now does so with mortgage debt still outstanding, according to the equity release advisers Key Retirement Solutions.

- Two-fifths of workers are failing to save for their retirement, highlighting the pensions 'time bomb' set to explode in the U.K.

- An analysis of pensioners' income in 2004 showed that only 68% of household income of 65–74 year olds is coming from pensions – state or private. For those aged 75 and over the percentage is 71%. The rest of the household income is from things like part-time jobs, other benefits, and investment income.

- Life expectancy is increasing. The average life expectancy of a male aged 65 is projected to be another 27.7 years by 2050.

- The average male retirement age was 67.2 in 1950, and fell to 63.1 by 1995.

- Only 53% of women are employed at the age of 59.

- There are approximately 11.3 million people now in work not making contributions to a personal pension scheme.

- The first report of the Pensions Commission published in 2004 said that spending on pensions – by government and individuals – will have to rise by £57 billion a year to maintain pensioners' present living standards at the then current levels.

- The same report said that as an alternative to increasing spending on pensions by £57 billion per year, the retirement age would have to be extended to 70.

Providing for yourself

The clear message is that you cannot rely on the State Pension in the same way as people have done in the past. In the future, you will have to rely more on your own private provision for your pensions. How do you do this?

The way to provide for a pension – particularly from your business – is what the rest of this book is dedicated to.

Quantifying the need

Before thinking about how to provide for your pension, the first step is to try to calculate how much you aspire to get as a pension in your retirement. Try following these steps, which are quite easy on a spreadsheet:

1   Enter your present income.
2   Enter the expected rate at which your income will increase until retirement.
3   Enter the number of years until retirement.
4   Enter the percentage of your final income which you expect to get as a pension.
5   Enter the expected rate of growth of your retirement fund.
6   Enter the expected annuity rate for a pension fund at your retirement date.
7   Use the 'future value' function on the spreadsheet to calculate your expected income at retirement date.
8   Multiply this by the percentage you have entered at step 4.
9   Divide this by the expected annuity rate you have entered at step 6, to arrive at the pension fund you will need to achieve your expected pension.

10   Use the 'payment' function on the spreadsheet to calculate the monthly payments you will need to save to achieve the pension fund, using the growth rate you have entered at step 5.

Example

1   Your present income is £20,000 per year.

2   You expect an increase of 4% per year.

3   You have 15 years until retirement.

4   You would like a pension of 50% of your final income.

5   You expect your retirement fund to grow at 5% per year.

6   You expect the annuity rate for pensions to be 7%.

7   The 'future value' function returns a final income figure of £36,019 at your expected retirement date.

8   Thus, you would expect a pension of £18,009 at that date.

9   To achieve this pension, you would need a pension fund of £257,258.

10 To achieve this fund you would need to save £958.55 per month starting now.

Simplification in 2006

In April 2006, the government has announced that there will be a 'simplification' of pensions, and in particular, the taxation treatment of pension savings.

At present, there are eight tax regimes for pension savings schemes which attract tax relief. These will be replaced by a single regime. Details of this simplification are given in Appendix 1.

CHECKLIST

- You must start to plan for retirement right now.
- You must take responsibility for your own future.
- Do the sums – work out how much you need to save for retirement if you want to maintain your lifestyle.

2
The State Pension provision

QUESTIONS, QUESTIONS

- Will my State Pension be adequate for my retirement?
- Will I need to supplement my State Pension with any other sort of income?
- Do I really need to provide my own pension on top of the State Pension?

Retirement Pension (The State Pension)

The State Pension is paid to people reaching the qualifying age. At present this is 60 for women and 65 for men, but this will be equalised (see section below). The State Pension consists of the following elements:

- Basic pension,
- Additional pension (also known as SERPS or State Second Pension),
- Graduated Retirement Benefit,
- Long-term Incapacity Benefit Age Addition,
- Age addition, and
- Extra pension for dependants.

Basic State Pension

The basic State Pension is dependent on National Insurance Contributions having been paid or credited. If you have not paid or been credited with sufficient contributions, you may have a chance to pay extra contributions to increase your entitlement. If you do not pay this extra, the basic pension is scaled down proportionately to the shortfall in your contributions.

If you have not paid or been credited with any contributions, you are not entitled to any State Pension, until you reach the age of 80. If you have not been employed or earning because you were bringing up children, or looking after a dependent relative, you may apply for Home Responsibilities Protection. This effectively reduces the number of years over which you were expected to make contributions, so that the full basic pension may be payable with a reduced number of years' contributions.

A married woman who does not qualify for the full basic State Pension based on her own contributions can receive the full basic pension based on her husband's contributions provided that:

- the husband is getting a basic pension, and
- the wife is aged at least 60.

A widow or widower may be able to get the basic pension and up to 50% of the additional pension based on their deceased spouse's contributions.

- A widow or widower may also get 100% of their

deceased spouse's SERPS or Additional State Pension when the spouse dies, if they reached State Pension age before 6 October 2002.

- If they reached State Pension age between 6 October 2002 and 5 October 2010, the maximum SERPS or S2P inherited by the widow or widower is between 90% and 100%.

- If they reach State Pension age after 5 October 2010, the widow or widower will receive a maximum of 50% of the SERPS or S2P.

A divorced person who does not qualify for full basic pension based on his or her contributions may be able to get the full basic pension based on their former spouse's contributions.

The basic State Pension is not affected by any earnings from working after your retirement date. However, a dependant's earnings will affect your extra pension for dependants (see below).

If you or your dependant spouse are in hospital for 52 weeks, the pension will be reduced.

The pension is still payable if you go to live abroad.

Additional State Pension
This is an addition to the basic pension and is dependent on earnings related National Insurance Contributions paid by employees (known as Class 1 contributions). From 1978 until 2002, these additional contributions were called the State Earnings Related Pension Scheme (SERPS). From 2002, they were known as State Second Pension (S2P).

For Class 1 National Insurance purposes, your earnings are classified into three tiers – the lower tier (up to the minimum level at which NI is charged), the middle tier (where earnings are subject to NI contributions), and the upper tier (where employers – but not employees – pay at a higher rate). The earnings related contributions are calculated by reference to the middle tier. The benefit is also based on the middle tier earnings.

Self employed people do pay Class 4 contributions, which are earnings related, but these do not qualify for any additional pension.

Graduated Retirement Benefit

This is based on contributions made by employed persons between April 1961 and April 1975 under the graduated scheme – it was a sort of earnings related scheme. For every £7.50 paid by men, and for every £9 paid by women under this scheme, the benefit is £9.63 per week.

Long-term Incapacity Benefit Age Addition

If you were receiving Long Term Incapacity Benefit at any time within eight weeks of reaching retirement age, you will receive the age addition to your pension. However, if you get any additional State Pension (i.e. any increase above the basic figure) this additional amount will automatically reduce the Long Term Incapacity Benefit Age Addition.

Age addition

When you reach the age of 80, an additional 25p per week is added to your pension.

Extra pension for dependants

Your basic pension is increased for your husband or wife. Benefits for children are now made through Child Tax Credits, but if you were receiving extra State Pension for children as dependants before 6 April 2003, this will continue to be paid in the same way. The benefit is £9.55 per week for the oldest qualifying child, and £11.35 per week for every other qualifying child.

Rates of State Pension

The amounts of pensions are reviewed every year and the new rates come into force on the first pay day after 5 April each year. For the year ended 5 April 2005, the weekly basic State Pension is:

- Based on your own or your deceased spouse's
  National Insurance Contributions   £79.60
- Based on your spouse's contributions   £47.65
- Non-contributory pension for over-80s   £47.65
- Extra pension for dependant spouse   £47.65

Deferring the State Pension

On reaching the State Pension age you do not have to take the pension immediately. You may defer the pension. The pension is then increased by 1% for every seven weeks you have deferred it. The increase is therefore approximately 7.5% for deferring it for a whole year. You may only defer the pension for a maximum of five years.

Claiming benefit

You will normally be sent a form to claim your pension four months before reaching State Pension age. If you have not received it within three months of that date, you should get in touch with the Pension Service.

Getting a pension forecast

On approaching your State Pension age, you may write to the Pension Service to get a forecast of the pension you should receive. That forecast will also tell you if your contributions are not sufficient to entitle you to the full pension, and how much you may pay as additional voluntary contributions to qualify you for the full basic pension.

Other benefits

The *Winter Fuel Payment* is paid to all people from age 60, regardless of whether they are receiving a pension or not.

A *Christmas Bonus* of £10 is paid in December to all pensioners.

Cold Weather Payments of £8.50 are made for each period of extreme cold weather, to all pensioners who are receiving the guarantee credit element of the Pension Credit (see below).

Free prescriptions and free eye tests are available to all people from age 60, regardless of whether they are receiving a pension or not.

Minimum Income Guarantee and The Pension Credit

The Minimum Income Guarantee was introduced in the 1999 budget, and finally became effective in October 2003. It was designed to reduce poverty amongst pensioners and also to reward people who have saved for retirement. The Pension Credit consists of two main elements:

Guarantee Credit. This ensures a minimum level of income for all people aged 60 and over.

Savings Credit. This provides extra income for people aged 65 and over who have made some provision for their retirement by having a small private pension or some savings in other forms.

People can qualify for both elements, or each element separately. This depends on the age and income of the claimant and partner.

The two elements work together so that entitlement is different for the age groups below.

Pension Credit from ages 60 to 64

For couples, only one partner needs to be 60. It guarantees a minimum level of income by topping up people's weekly income. It is available to people with incomes below the following limits:

- Single person   £105.45 per week (for the 2004/2005 tax year).

- Couples   £160.95 per week (for the 2004/2005 tax year).

However, if the claimants are:

- severely disabled, or
- looking after a person who is severely disabled, or
- have housing costs such as mortgage interest payments,

then the income limit is raised.

The Credit works simply by topping up the income to the figures given above.

Pension Credit from age 65 onwards

For couples, only one partner needs to be 65. This is available to people with incomes below the following limits:

- Single person   £144.00 per week (for the 2004/2005 tax year).
- Couples   £212.00 per week (for the 2004/2005 tax year).

However, if the claimants are:

- severely disabled, or
- looking after a person who is severely disabled, or
- have housing costs such as mortgage interest payments,

then the income limit is raised.

From age 65 onwards, the Savings Credit rewards pensioners

who have contributed to a second pension scheme or who have savings. The extent of this reward is 60p for every £1 for income above the level of the basic State Pension, with a maximum of £15.51 per week for a single person and £20.22 per week for a couple (for the 2004/2005 tax year).

The formula for working out the weekly Pension Credit for the 2004/2005 tax year is as follows:

- Where the income does not exceed the full basic rate of State Pension, the pension credit is:
  Single person   £105.45 less actual income.
  Couple   £160.95 less actual income.
- Where the income exceeds the full basic rate of State Pension, the pension credit is:
  Single person   (£105.45 less actual income) +
                    [0.6 x (actual income less £79.60)].
  Couple   (£160.95 less actual income) +
                    [0.6 x (actual income less £127.25)].

The Pension Credit depends on the claimant's income. Therefore, any changes in income must be reported to the Pension Service. However, if the claimant (and their partner if claiming as a couple) is or are both over 65, the retirement income for the purposes of calculation of the Pension Credit is fixed for five years. This is called the Assessed Income Period (AIP). Retirement income for these purposes is defined as:

- any private pensions from an employer's scheme or private scheme,
- annuities, and
- income from savings and investments.

However, if the income other than retirement income changes, then this must be reported to the Pension Service, even if it is in the five year period. If the claimant's income is reduced at any time, they can ask for a reassessment.

Other events which must be reported to the Pension Service are:

- Change in marital status or co-habitation status.
- The claimant or partner reaching the age of 65.
- No longer satisfying a condition of the Pension Credit.
- Retirement income reduces or is ceased temporarily.
- Entering a care home other than temporarily.

Equalisation of retirement ages

From 6 April 2020, the State Pension age will be 65 for both men and women. The age for women will start to change gradually from 2010.

Thus, women born before 6 April 1950 will not be affected. Their State Pension age will continue to be 60. The gradual changes will affect women born between 6 April 1950 and 5 April 1955. Women born after that date will have a State Pension age of 65.

CHECKLIST

- The basic State Pension is not enough to live on.
- There can be entitlement to additional State Pension.
- You can defer taking your State Pension.
- You can get a forecast of what your State Pension is

likely to be.

- Other benefits are available when you are of retirement age.
- The Pension credit is also available.
- Men's and women's retirement ages will be equalised.

Case study

Derek

Derek was employed for the first 10 years of his working life, then set up in his own business as a self employed person. As he approaches his retirement, he writes to the Benefits Agency to get a retirement pension forecast. He is devastated that his pension is not going to be nearly as much as he hoped. This is because he only paid the earnings related contributions for a relatively short period. Since being self-employed, he has paid class 2 and class 4 contributions.

He mistakenly thought that the class 4 contributions, being earnings-related, would qualify him for extra pension, and therefore has not provided nearly enough for a private pension. He decides that he will have to carry on working for a few extra years, and put more away in savings and a private pension scheme. During this extra working period, he decides to defer his State Pension to increase the value of it when he does retire.

3
Personal Pension schemes

- Can anybody take out a Personal Pension Plan, or are there restrictions?
- How do I choose between the large number of plans being marketed?
- How do I take the benefits when I retire?
- What other benefits are there (e.g. on death before pension age)?

Personal Pension schemes are plans, approved by the Inland Revenue, and run by insurance and pension companies, which are long term savings schemes, designed to provide for retirement. Because of the generous tax advantages, they have rules that must be adhered to in order to qualify for the tax concessions.

Eligibility and Qualifying Earnings

Anyone may contribute up to £3,600 per year gross (£2,808 net at current tax rates) to a Personal Pension Plan. If you want to contribute above this limit, you must have qualifying earnings to be able to put your money into one of these schemes. This means that your earnings must come from:

- self employment, or
- employment with an employer which does not have a pension scheme of its own, or
- furnished holiday letting income.

If you do not have earnings which qualify, the Inland Revenue can instruct the Pension company to repay to you any contributions you have paid.

Concurrency

An individual may pay contributions to a Personal Pension Plan as well as paying contributions to an occupational pension scheme at the same time. This is known as concurrency.

Contributions and tax relief

Contributions to a Personal Pension Plan are regulated, because the contributions benefit from tax relief.

Limits of contributions

The maximum limits of contributions to Personal Pension Plans are expressed as a percentage of the taxable income from the sources of income listed above in any tax year. The limits are as follows:

Age at *start* of tax year	Maximum percentage of earnings
35 or less	17.5%
36–45	20%
46–50	25%
51–55	30%
56–60	35%
61–74	40%

Note that the age is at the *start* of the tax year. There is also an overall limit to the contributions which may be paid in any tax year. This limit is the relevant percentage according to the table above, on the 'earnings cap'. The earnings cap is currently £105,600.

Basis year

There are very generous rules allowing you to make contributions based on your best year's earnings in any of the past five years. The best year's earnings can be nominated as your 'basis year'. This is also sometimes known as 'benchmarking'. Note however that the earnings must be the 'Net Relevant Earnings' for the basis year – i.e. they cannot be earnings when you were a member of an occupational pension scheme. They must be the earnings which qualify you to contribute to a Personal Pension Scheme.

The rules are very generous because:

- The earnings are based on the year you nominate.
- The age used as the basis for the percentage of earnings is the age at the beginning of the year of payment of contribution.
- The earnings cap is based on the year of payment of the contribution.

Any contributions made in the basis year do not affect the maximum limit in the year of payment.

Example

A man aged 61 has earnings for the 2004/2005 tax year of £15,000. In the tax year 2000/2001, he had earnings of £50,000. He may nominate 2000/2001 as his 'basis year'. He may then make pension contributions for 2004/2005 based on that £50,000. This means that he can contribute a maximum of 40% of £50,000 – i.e. £20,000 gross (£15,600 net of basic rate tax).

What is more, he can also make additional contributions for any of the five years from 2000/2001 to 2005/2006 based on the £50,000 earnings. Thus, for 2004/2005 and 2005/2006, he can make contributions of up to 40% of the £50,000, but for the earlier years, because he was under 61, he can make contributions up to 35% of the £50,000.

TIP FOR OWNER-DIRECTORS

Because of the ability to nominate a basis year, you can increase your salary in one year, and use this as the basis of your pension contributions for the next five years, regardless of your actual salary during those five years. During those years, you can take advantage of remunerating yourself by dividends, which often provide a more tax efficient way of remuneration. After five years, repeat the cycle to allow yourself to make substantial pension provision. This can often be particularly advantageous as you approach retirement age.

Tax relief

All contributions are made to the pension provider net of the basic rate of income tax, presently 22%. Thus, if a person pays £780, they will have the extra £220 paid by the government, so that the total credited to their pension plan is £1,000. This tax relief is given to all individuals, whether or not they are actually tax payers. In practice, this would only happen up to the £3,600 limit. Thus, if someone has no tax liability at all, they still only pay the net amount, and for every £78 paid, the government contributes the notional tax relief of £22.

If the person is a higher rate tax payer, the extra tax relief has to be claimed on the self assessment tax return each year. The additional tax (presently 18%) will then be refunded by way of a coding notice adjustment for directors and employees, or by the self-assessed tax paid by self-employed people. It can alternatively be claimed by completing an Inland Revenue form PP120.

TOP TIP

How to get extra tax relief from pension contributions

There is a special deadline in the tax calendar. 31 January is a deadline for submitting the previous year's self assessment tax return, but it is also the deadline for backdating pension contributions for tax purposes.

Any contribution paid before 31 January may be carried back to the previous tax year provided that an election to do this is made before or at the same time as the payment. (This is an irrevocable election). This can be useful for the extra tax relief which may be available if, for example, you were a higher rate taxpayer in the previous year. It could also be useful where you have already paid the maximum contributions for the current year, but have available allowance in the previous year.

However, there could be additional benefits in relation to tax credits. There are Child Tax Credits and Working Tax Credits. The entitlement to these credits is reduced if your total income is above the relevant thresholds. This reduction is known as abatement. The level of income for one tax year determines the amount of Tax Credit for the following year. Pension contributions reduce the income for these purposes, in the same way as for Income Tax purposes. For the purposes of Child Tax Credit, the income limit at the time of writing is £50,000. Extra Tax Credit could be achieved by carrying back pension contributions to reduce or eliminate the abatement in the previous tax year.

Example

Mr. and Mrs. Smith have an annual income of £57,000 for the 2003/2004 tax year. They pay regular pension contributions of £2,000 (gross) a year. Thus, for Child Tax Credit purposes their income is £55,000. This is £5,000 over the £50,000 limit. The abatement of Child Tax Credit is 1/15 of this excess – i.e. £333.33.

Now, if Mr. Smith pays an additional pension contribution before 31 January 2005 of £3,900 net, this equates to £5,000 gross. He can carry this back from the 2004/2005 tax year to the 2003/2004 tax year. The couple's income for 2003/2004 is now £50,000, and there is no abatement. The 2004/2005 Child Tax Credit is therefore now adjusted by paying an additional £333.33. This has effectively reduced the cost of the extra pension contribution.

You may make a special election to carry back contributions paid in a tax year to the previous tax year, as long as the limits of contributions in the previous tax year are not exceeded. Making this special election is beneficial if the rate of tax paid in the previous year was higher than the current year – for example, by paying the higher rate of tax. This election is made by completing Inland Revenue form PP43.

Excess contributions

If a person has paid contributions in excess of the maximum allowable amounts for tax purposes, the pension provider must pay back the excess. The net amount is paid to the individual, and the excess tax relief is repaid to the government.

Taking the benefits

The main condition of Personal Pension Schemes is that the benefits can only be paid between the ages of 50 and 75. There are, however, several categories of occupation which allow earlier retirement for the purposes of drawing benefits. These include many sports activities, such as wrestlers, downhill skiers, footballers, jockeys, etc. Some other types of occupation, such as models and dancers, are also included in the list.

The pension you receive is an annuity purchased by your fund. An annuity is a regular sum, paid monthly, quarterly, or annually, for the rest of your life.

The two factors affecting the amount of pension are therefore:

- the size of the fund, and
- the annuity rate.

The annuity rate represents the factor used to convert the fund into a pension. The annuity rate calculation consists of two elements:

1   The interest element, based on long-term government securities.
2   The capital element, based on the life expectancy of the annuitant.

It is worked out by actuaries using up to date information on rates of mortality, interest rates, and the age and gender of the person. The state of health of the person can also influence the annuity rate (see impaired life annuities below).

Types of annuities

- Annuities can be of fixed amounts (i.e. non-increasing), or increasing amounts.
- The increases can be of a fixed amount each year (generally 3% or 5%), or linked to the retail prices index.
- Investment linked annuities (either 'with profit' or 'unit linked') pay variable annuities, linked to the performance of the underlying investments.
- Annuities can be for the sole life of the beneficiary (known as a single life annuity), or for the joint lives of the beneficiary and his or her spouse.
- A minimum guarantee period of, say, five or ten years can be provided if requested. This means that if the beneficiary dies within that period, the survivors get the income for the rest of that guarantee period.
- The frequency of payment can marginally affect the amount of the annuity. If they are paid less frequently (e.g. quarterly, half yearly or yearly rather than monthly), they are generally slightly higher, and if they are paid in arrears rather than in advance, they are generally slightly higher.
- There are also 'impaired life' annuities. This means that if the beneficiary is suffering from a life-threatening illness, then because the life span is not expected to be so long, the annuity rate is increased.

- There are also some innovative annuity products offered by some pension providers, such as:
  Flexible annuity, which allows the fund to be invested in collective investments (such as unit trust or investment trusts) instead of government securities. There is an option to convert to a conventional annuity, and part of the fund can be retained if the annuitant dies within 10 years, to be passed to the annuitant's survivors.
  Open annuity, in which the fund is invested in shares in the insurance company, and the balance of the fund remains repayable to the estate on the death of the annuitant. This is offered currently by an offshore life assurance company.
- An annuity growth account offers the annuitant the chance to buy a temporary five year annuity, and the balance of the funds is invested in growth investments. When the five years are over, the annuitant can buy another temporary annuity, or a lifetime annuity from the proceeds of the growth funds.

Death Benefit

If you die before taking the retirement benefits, then the pension policy will state what benefit your dependants will receive. In some older retirement annuity policies, the death benefit was only a return of contributions, with or without a nominal rate of interest. Currently, the best practice is for the value of the accumulated fund to be paid as the death benefit. This is certainly one of the key points to look for in a policy.

Tax Free Lump Sum

When you take your pension, you need not take all of it in the form of a regular pension. Part of the fund may be taken as a tax-free lump sum. At present, the regulations allow you to take up to 25% of the fund as a lump sum. This fund is technically known as the non-Protected Rights fund.

It is nearly always beneficial to take this lump sum. This allows you to invest the lump sum, enjoy the income, and still have the capital available if you need it, or to pass on to your survivors. Clearly this is better; otherwise the whole fund is tied up in the annuity, and there is no access to the capital.

Open Market Option

When the policy matures, and you want to take your pension, you have the right to take the fund from your pension company, and 'shop around' for the best value pension. This is because the pension offered by each company is determined by its own annuity rates. These rates vary, and shopping around enables you to find the best value. This 'Open Market Option' must be written into the pension contract to enable it to qualify for the tax advantages. The pension company must inform you of this option on the maturity of the policy.

Phased retirement

You may phase in your retirement if you wish to start reducing your working time gradually over a period of a few years. This can be done by dividing the Personal Pension scheme into a number of different policies. Then, the benefits can start to be drawn one at a time, so that the retirement benefits gradually increase, as the earnings from work gradually tail off.

Example

George has a personal pension scheme into which he contributes every month. However, instead of the scheme consisting of one policy, it consists of ten equal policies. George decides to reduce his working time from age 55, by working four days a week, and gradually reducing that by a further day a week until age 60 when he retires completely.

As his income gradually reduces from his work, he starts to take the benefits from his personal pension scheme, by taking the benefits from two policies per year each year for the five years over which he reduces his working week. Thus, his income is evened out.

Income Drawdown

When annuity rates are not high, (and particularly if this also occurs at a time when the value of the fund may be low due to prevailing investment conditions) it may be disadvantageous to take the annuity. This is because, once the annuity is taken, the benefits are 'locked in' to the prevailing interest rates and investment conditions.

An income drawdown plan overcomes this problem. This type of plan allows the fund to remain in place, and continue earning income and benefiting from any investment growth. In the meantime, an 'income' may be drawn from the fund. Although this income is liable to tax, it is strictly speaking a drawing on the capital of the fund. The beneficiary may also choose to use a part of the fund to buy an annuity in the normal way, and use the balance for a drawdown scheme.

The amount which may be so drawn down is regulated, and depends on the age of the beneficiary, and the size of the fund.

It is also subject to review every three years. The limits are:

- Maximum limit – equal to a single life annuity, non-increasing, with no guarantees.
- Minimum limit – 35% of the maximum limit.

The benefit of this plan is that the fund remains in existence.

If the beneficiary dies before taking an annuity:

- The fund can be paid to the beneficiary's estate. This is subject to a tax charge of 35%.
- The survivor can continue to draw down from the fund, but only until the original member would have reached age 75 at the latest.
- The fund can be used to buy an annuity for the survivor.

This type of plan may only be in existence until at latest the beneficiary reaches the age of 75. At that time, the fund must be converted into an annuity.

Choosing a policy

If you are considering taking out a policy, there is a bewildering number of choices available, and an equally bewildering number of salesmen trying to sell them to you. Bear in mind that they are earning their living, in the form of commission on these policies. The adviser you use may be independent or an employee of the company, but they still have a living to earn. Some companies advertise the fact that they do not pay commission to intermediaries. However, they still have their own sales force to pay.

However, the fact that a salesman gets commission does not necessarily mean that what they are trying to sell you is not good value.

Here are some points to look for when choosing a pension:

What is the basis of the fund growth?

The funds are usually unit linked or with profit.

Unit linked means that the premiums buy you a certain number of units in a fund or funds provided by the pension company. Like Unit Trusts, there are various types of funds. The prices are quoted in the financial press, and the value of your pension fund at any time is the value of the units, multiplied by the number of units you hold. This means, of course, that the value can fall as well as rise.

With profit funds mean that the investment profits each year are credited to your account, as a 'bonus declaration'. The bonuses are added to the value of your fund each year, and there is also usually a 'terminal bonus' added when the policy matures. The annual bonuses cannot be taken away once they have been added to your fund. Although it may seem preferable to have profits added in this way, the 'with profit' policies usually keep a reserve back in good years to even out the growth.

What is the charging structure?

Many companies pay commission, and, particularly in the case of regular premium policies, this means there is a large deduction from your fund in the first year or two. Thus, it could take your fund a long time to recuperate from this reduction. This is known as 'front end loading'.

How flexible is the policy?

Do you want to pay regular premiums, or a single premium? Does your policy give you the opportunity to suspend premiums if necessary? If you are paying regular monthly or yearly premiums, can you add on single premiums at a later date?

What is the basis of the benefit if you should die before taking the pension?

You should always look for the fund value as the benefit, rather than return of premiums, even with interest.

Group Personal Pension Plans

An employer may offer to employees the benefits of a Group Personal Pension Plan. Under this arrangement, a pension provider typically offers better terms to a collection of plans grouped together under one employer. Although the administrative work is done by the employer, the individual contracts are between the individuals and the pension provider.

An employer may use this type of plan as an alternative to offering a stakeholder pension scheme. If so, the employer must contribute at least 3% of the basic salary of employees to the plans.

Retirement Annuity Plans

These plans were the precursors to Personal Pension Plans. They are no longer available as new plans, but existing plans continue in force. See more detail about these plans in Chapter 7.

CHECKLIST

- You should have qualifying earnings to take out a personal pension plan above a certain limit.
- You can nominate a 'basis year' to maximise your contributions (known as 'benchmarking').
- You get tax relief on your contributions.
- You can take out a tax free lump sum on retirement.
- You do not have to take the pension with the same company you saved with – use the Open Market Option.
- You have many options of how to take the pension itself.
- You can phase your retirement, or use the drawdown option if applicable.

Case study

Alan chooses a plan

Alan is self-employed and in his mid 20s, and has taken advice to start making provision for his retirement. As he has a long time to go before his retirement, he does not want to invest too large an amount in contributions – he wants to save up for a deposit on a house. Having decided on a modest sum of £40 per month to start with, he goes to an independent financial adviser to choose a pension provider for a Personal Pension Plan. He believes that a mutual society would best serve his long-term needs, as he would become a member by taking out a policy, and share in the profits. Also, if they decided to demutualise, he might be in line for a windfall.

Having taken advice, he chooses to have his funds invested in equities, since he believes that will give the best long-term return on his investment. He then makes a mental note to review the investments when he is about two or three years off retirement, with a view to switching them to a fixed interest investment so as to preserve the capital value from any short-term fluctuation in value and any possible losses.

4
Stakeholder Pensions

QUESTIONS, QUESTIONS

- Who can take out a Stakeholder Pension?
- What are the benefits of Stakeholder Pensions?
- What tax relief do they give on contributions?
- Can I make contributions to Stakeholder Pensions when I am employed?

Stakeholder Pensions are available to practically everybody, and can be a more economical way of contributing to retirement saving. They are currently offered by many insurance companies, banks, investment houses, and some retailers offering financial services. They may also be offered by some employers, since all employers with more than five employees had to offer access to a Stakeholder Pension if they did not have any other pension arrangements for their employees by 8 October 2001.

Individuals may take out Stakeholder Pensions for:

- themselves,
- their spouses, and
- their children. Any plan taken out for a child reverts to them when they reach the age of 18.

Eligibility

A stakeholder pension is available to almost anyone as a means of saving for retirement. It is available regardless of status such as:

- Employed.
- Self employed.
- Not employed.
- Tax payer.
- Not a tax payer.

The only qualifications that apply to Stakeholder Pensions are:

- the contributor must be under 75 years of age, and
- the contributor must be resident in the U.K.

Tax Relief

- Basic rate tax relief is given at source on all contributions to Stakeholder Pensions.
- Even if an individual is not a taxpayer, they still get the benefit of tax relief.
- This is done by means of paying the contributions at a 'net of tax' rate, and the government refunding to the pension providing company the tax rebate. Thus, for every £78 contributed by an individual at the present basic rate of tax, the government contributes £22.
- If the contributor is a higher rate tax payer, relief is given by the annual self assessment.

Minimum Standards

The government has set down certain minimum standards for a scheme to be accepted as a Stakeholder Pension:

- The charges cannot exceed 1% per year of the member's fund (and there are no initial charges).
- No penalties are allowed on:
  transferring the benefits to another scheme, or
  stopping contributions to the fund.
- The minimum contribution to a plan may not be set at more than £20 per period – whether as a regular payment or a one-off payment.
- There must be a default fund for members who do not wish to make investment decisions.
- Statements must be issued at least annually.
- Up to 10% of the fund can be used as a life assurance premium.
- The scheme must allow for the option of up to 25% of the fund to be taken as a tax-free lump sum at retirement.
- Retirement must be between the ages of 50 and 75.

Many of these standards apply also to Personal Pension Plans, but some of these standards mean that Stakeholder Pensions are cheaper than Personal Pension Plans.

Contributions

Everyone who is eligible may pay contributions up to the current earnings threshold (which is currently £3,600 gross) regardless of earnings. Thus, the actual maximum amount after the tax relief at source is £2,808 at current tax rates.

Higher amounts are allowable related to the earnings and the age of the contributor as follows:

Age	Percentage of earnings
up to 35	17.5%
36–45	20%
46–51	25%
51–55	30%
56–60	35%
61–74	40%

This is subject to an overall earnings cap (currently of £105,600 per year).

Nomination of a basis year ('benchmarking') is available for Stakeholder Pensions as for Personal Pension Plans (see Chapter 3).

Concurrency

This term means that you may contribute to a Stakeholder Pension at the same time as other schemes, or even another Stakeholder Pension. Overall contributions in any tax year must however be kept within the limits described above. The rules depend on what type of other scheme is involved.

Occupational scheme

There are three types of occupational schemes:

- **New regime schemes**. These schemes are treated for

concurrency purposes like Personal Pension Plans. Stakeholder Pensions may be paid concurrently.

- **Old regime schemes**. These schemes only allow concurrency for people who are:
  - not controlling directors, and
  - whose earnings after deducting pension contributions are £30,000 p.a. or less in at least one of the preceding five tax years.

N.B. If you are in doubt as to the category of your occupational scheme, the Inland Revenue or your plan administrator can advise you.

- **Scheme providing lump sum payment on death only**. Concurrency is allowed up to a maximum of the greater of:
  - £3,600 per year gross (£2,808 net), or
  - 15% of earnings.

Personal Pension Plan

Concurrency is permissible, but total contributions must not exceed the limits described above.

Another Stakeholder Pension

You may be in as many Stakeholder Pension Plans as you like, but the total contributions in any tax year must not exceed the limits described above.

Employer Stakeholder Schemes

Employers are obliged to offer at least Stakeholder Schemes to relevant employees unless they have fewer than five employees.

Relevant employees are all employees *except* the following:

- Those who have worked for the employer less than three months.
- Those who are members of the employer's occupational scheme.
- Those who have declined to join the occupational scheme.
- Those who have earned less than the Income Threshold for National Insurance purposes for at least one week in the last three months.
- Those ineligible to join Stakeholder schemes.

If the employer sets up a Stakeholder scheme, they must:

- Choose a Stakeholder scheme from the OPRA register.
- Discuss the choice with employees or their representatives.
- Communicate the name and address of the scheme to all relevant employees or their representatives.
- Arrange for payroll deductions of contributions for all those employees choosing to join the scheme.
- Send all contributions (employer and employee) to the Stakeholder provider, maintaining proper records of this.
- Offer access to the scheme to all employees when they complete three months' employment.

CHECKLIST

- Stakeholder Pensions are available to anyone regardless of employment status, or level of earnings.
- Full tax relief is available on contributions.
- 'Benchmarking' of a basis year is available.
- Government standards mean that they can be cheaper than Personal Pension schemes.
- You can contribute to them at the same time as other schemes.
- Employers may offer group Stakeholder schemes.

Case study

Norah

Norah is just starting a self-employed business. She is in her early 30s, and the first few years of her self employment are not likely to be highly profitable. She fully intends to make provision for her retirement, but knows that she will not be able to afford to pay high amounts in premiums until a few years down the line. It is also possible that she may not be paying tax in the first couple of years – at least, not the basic rate of tax.

Norah decides therefore to make contributions to a Stakeholder Pension, contributing only £780 in her first year, which is made up to £1,000 by the government. The cheaper charges on a Stakeholder Pension means that she should get better value on her relatively low contributions. She plans gradually to increase her contributions over a few years, and then perhaps take out a Personal Pension Plan.

5
Occupational Schemes

QUESTIONS, QUESTIONS

- Is an Occupational Scheme better than a Personal Pension Plan?
- Do employers have to provide Occupational Schemes?
- How does an Occupational Scheme have to be set up and run?
- Do employers have to contribute to employees' pensions?
- What tax advantages are there for the company and the employee?
- What is the difference between a Final Salary Scheme and a Money Purchase Scheme?
- Can I contribute to other schemes at the same time as an Occupational Scheme?
- Can I transfer an Occupational Pension Scheme to a new employer?
- How can I take the benefits from an Occupational Scheme?
- What is so special about Executive Pension Plans?

Employers are under an obligation to offer at least Stakeholder Pensions to their employees (but they are not under an obligation to make contributions) if they have at least five employees (see Chapter 4). Alternatives to this include group Personal Pension Schemes or Occupational Schemes.

Occupational Schemes

These are schemes set up by and sponsored by employers. The actual scheme is, however, run by a board of trustees, who are independent of the employer, and are there to ensure that the benefits under the scheme are properly funded and actually paid out. They also ensure that the pension funds are kept separate from the business's own money.

Employers *must* contribute to occupational schemes, but employees are not obliged to contribute. Schemes in which only the employer contributes are known as 'non-contributory schemes'.

The scheme must be approved by the Inland Revenue, which has a dedicated office, the Pension Schemes Office (PSO) for this purpose.

There are two main types of occupational schemes:

1   Final Salary Schemes, and
2   Money Purchase Schemes.

Tax advantages

Approved Occupational Schemes enjoy considerable tax benefits. To take advantage of these tax benefits, the trust deed and the rules must comply with Inland Revenue requirements. A summary of the requirements in terms of the limits imposed is given in Appendix 2.

The tax benefits include exemptions from:

- Income Tax on all income from investments and deposits, (but see exception below).
- Income Tax on underwriting.
- Capital Gains Tax.
- Income Tax on lump sums at retirement.
- Corporation Tax for the employer's contributions.
- Income Tax for the employees' contributions.

However, Income Tax *is* payable on:

- Dividend income in the scheme's fund.
- Refund of pension scheme contributions, at 20%.
- Refund of surplus AVCs and FSAVCs, at 32%.
- Commutation of pension into a lump sum, when the excess of the lump sum over the maximum allowable tax-free lump sum is taxed at 20%.

Final Salary Schemes

These schemes are also sometimes referred to as 'defined benefit' schemes, or 'salary related' schemes. Contributions are made to the scheme by employers and employees, in an agreed proportion. The benefits payable under the scheme are related to three elements:

1   The length of service by the employee in the scheme.
2   The earnings at retirement date (known as final pension-able salary).
3   The scheme's 'accrual rate'. This is the proportion of the final salary paid as benefit for each year of service.

Example

The accrual rate is 1/60 of the final salary for every year of service.

The member had 30 years' service.

The member's final salary was £35,000 per year.

The benefit (i.e. pension) would be 30/60, or one half the final salary – i.e. £17,500 per year.

It is usual to allow an employee to remain as an active member during a temporary absence. This may be due to illness, or taking a sabbatical. The maximum period of temporary absence allowed is 30 months. During this period of temporary absence, the member's retirement benefits continue to accrue, and the member is covered for death in service benefits.

Money Purchase Schemes

These are sometimes referred to as 'defined contribution' schemes. Contributions are made to the scheme by employers and employees, in an agreed proportion. The money is invested in a specific fund for each member. The benefits under the scheme depend on:

1   The amount paid into the pension fund.
2   How well the investment performs.
3   The annuity rate at the date of retirement.

One feature of a Money Purchase Scheme is that the tax free lump sum may be drawn up to the maximum permitted by the rules or the Inland Revenue limits. Only the balance of the fund is then used to provide an annuity.

In a Money Purchase Scheme, the employer must contribute at least 10% of the total contributions.

Simplified Defined Contribution Schemes (SDCS)

These schemes are not very common. They are, as the name implies, a money purchase type of scheme. Further restrictions apply, including:

- Membership is not allowed to a director holding 20% or more of the voting power of a company.
- Concurrent membership is not allowed except to an FSAVC (see below).

The maximum contribution for an employee into an SDCS is 15%, but the maximum combined contribution of employer and employee is 17.5%, of which 5% may go towards a lump sum death benefit. Up to 25% of the fund at retirement may be used to pay a tax free lump sum.

Hybrid Schemes

A hybrid scheme combines elements of Final Salary Schemes and Money Purchase Schemes. The calculation of the benefits is based on money purchase and final salary basis. So, if the member retires or leaves the scheme early, the member will receive a fund or an income, whichever is the greater. This type of scheme can provide more security of benefits linked to salary, and often means that the member is less likely to lose benefits on leaving the scheme early, whatever the reason.

Contribution limits

All contributions to an Occupational Pension Scheme that is approved by the Inland Revenue receive full tax relief at the top rate of tax paid. This applies to all contributions made – from employees and from the employer.

Because of this tax-advantaged status, there are limits on the amounts which may be contributed. Employees may contribute up to 15% of their total remuneration in any tax year. For these purposes, the remuneration includes:

• Normal pay taxed under PAYE.
• Benefits charged to tax (such as company cars, medical insurance, etc.).
• Profit related pay.
• Amounts used to purchase partnership shares in share incentive plans.

The remuneration, however, excludes:

• Golden handshakes.
• Share option gains.

There is an overall earnings cap which applies to the earnings for the purpose of calculating the 15% limit. For the current tax year (2005/2006) the earnings cap is £105,600. Therefore, the maximum any employee could contribute in the current tax year is 15% of £105,600 – or £15,840.

The employer may also make contributions to the scheme on behalf of employees. In fact, the contribution of employers is a condition of approval of a scheme by the Inland Revenue.

The contributions of the employer are not limited to a maximum, but there is a lower contribution limit of 10% of the total contributions to the scheme (i.e. employees and employer together) in any tax year.

Payment of contributions

Employees' contributions to an Occupational Scheme must be paid over to the trustees by the 19th of the month following the month in which the contributions were deducted from the pay of the employees.

Example
Deductions from the pay in September 2005 must be paid to the trustees by 19 October 2005.

The trustees of the scheme must monitor the prompt payment of contributions. If payment is made late, the trustees must:

- report the non-payment or late payment to the Occupational Pensions Regulatory Authority (OPRA) within 30 days of the due date, and
- report to the members of the scheme if the contributions have still not been paid after 60 days from the due date.

However, the trustees need not report the late payment:

- if the payment is made within 10 days of the due date, and
- late payment has not happened previously more than once.

Employer's contributions dates are made at their discretion, but once a regular date has been fixed, it must be adhered to, and the trustees must monitor this also.

Members' contributions to other schemes

Members of Occupational Schemes are not limited to making all their retirement provision by their employer's scheme. Extra contributions may be made by:

- Additional Voluntary Contributions (AVCs), or
- Free Standing Additional Voluntary Contributions (FSAVCs), or
- Concurrency provisions (see Chapter 4).

AVCs (Additional Voluntary Contributions)

To obtain the approved exempt status for tax purposes, Occupational Schemes must offer to the members the ability to pay AVCs – i.e. additional contributions into the same scheme. These allow the members the opportunity to contribute extra money to top up their retirement fund. AVCs do not usually benefit from any matching contribution from the employer, whereas the normal contributions often do.

The contributions paid into AVCs are nearly always Money Purchase Schemes, even if the main Occupational Scheme is a Final Salary Scheme. AVCs are also usually negotiated by the trustees of the scheme with the pension provider at low cost or no cost. Contributions to AVCs enjoy the same tax relief as normal contributions, always subject, however, to the normal 15% limit and the earnings cap. The trustees of the scheme are responsible for ensuring that the limits are not breached. If the limit is breached however, a refund of excess AVC contributions is paid to the member, subject to a tax charge of 33% if the member is a basic rate tax payer, or 48% if the member is a higher rate tax payer.

> **Example**
> Mr. A. Contributor has put 6% of his earnings into his employer's occupational scheme. He may put up to 9% in an AVC.

AVC contributions may be used to provide additional pension (and the Open Market Option is available for AVCs), or, in certain circumstances, to buy extra years of service within a final salary pension scheme. Either benefit may be taken within the normal retirement dates applying to pension schemes – between age 50 and age 75. They do not have to be taken at the same time as the benefits from the main scheme (providing that the Occupational Pension Scheme rules allow this).

AVCs may not be used to provide a tax-free lump sum (unless the arrangement was in place before 8 April 1987). AVCs are a good way to make up any shortfall in retirement funds due to breaks in service, or early retirement.

FSAVCs (Free Standing Additional Voluntary Contributions)

FSAVCs are a way of contributing additional amounts to a retirement fund outside of the Occupational Scheme. In other words, a member of an Occupational Scheme may make additional contributions to any other provider he wishes, outside of the employer's Occupational Scheme. FSAVCs are only available to people who are members of an Occupational Scheme. Because FSAVCs are not included in the sponsored AVCs of the employer's scheme, they would normally be expected to bear extra costs, both initial set up costs and annual charges.

FSAVCs are also subject to the same overall limits as AVCs – 15% of earnings subject to the earnings cap. The responsibility for ensuring that the limits are not breached is with the provider of the FSAVC.

Example
Mr. B. Contributor has paid 6% of his earnings into his employer's occupational scheme, and a further 4% into an AVC. He may therefore put up to a further 5% into a FSAVC.

FSAVCs enjoy the same tax advantages as AVCs.

- FSAVCs may only be used to provide additional pension.
- The benefit may be taken within the normal retirement dates applying to pension schemes – between age 50 and age 75.
- They do not have to be taken at the same time as the benefits from the main scheme (providing that the Occupational Pension Scheme rules allow this).

FSAVCs may seem to have disadvantages, but their advantages are:

- The contributor can choose the company into which the money is invested, and the type of investment.

- The contributor may continue to pay into it even if there is a change of Occupational Scheme, or if he changes employer.

Concurrency

As we have seen in Chapter 4, concurrency means the ability to contribute to more than one type of pension provision, provided generally that the overall limits are observed (i.e. 15% of earnings up to the earnings limit). An Occupational Scheme member may contribute to a Personal Pension Plan or a Stakeholder Pension provided that:

- he has not been a controlling director of the employer in any of the past five years, and
- he has earned less than the remuneration limit (currently £30,000 plus the value of the member's annual contributions to the Occupational Scheme) in any one of the last five years.

If the member of an Occupational Scheme takes advantage of the concurrency provisions, the maximum contributions to a Personal Pension Plan or Stakeholder Pension are £3,600 per year gross (£2,808 net) at current tax rates.

Benefits

Retirement benefits

The official retirement age of the scheme is known as the NRA (Normal Retirement Age), and this must be set between the ages of 60 and 75. However, benefits may be drawn earlier than the NRA, at any time between the ages of 50 and 75. See

Chapter 7 for details of early retirement on ill health grounds.

Earlier ages are eligible for NRA for certain occupations, including:

- Airline pilots.
- Distant Water Trawlermen.
- Money Brokers.
- Models.
- Professional Footballers.

Maximum benefits of retirement pensions are:

- $\frac{2}{3}$ of final remuneration, subject to the number of years' service, and the earnings cap (currently £105,600 p.a.). However, this pension may escalate in retirement.
- Some of the pension may be commuted to a tax free lump sum of 150% of final remuneration.

Death Benefits

Occupational Schemes must provide for death benefits to dependants. Dependants can be wives, husbands or children under the age of 18, even if they are not financially dependent on the member. A dependant can also be an unmarried partner of the member, including same-sex partners.

These benefits vary according to the status of the member at the time of death:

- Active members (death in service).
- Deferred members.
- Pensioners.

Active members

The death benefit is similar to a life assurance policy. The death benefit is related to the member's salary at the time of death. The maximum benefit allowable for the scheme to be approved by the Inland Revenue is four times the salary at the time of death. This is a tax free lump sum. The member will have had to state who they would like the death benefit paid to. However, the trustees have the final authority as to who is paid the death benefit.

For Final Salary Schemes the normal death benefit is the refund of the member's contributions. The rules can provide for a pension to the surviving spouse of up to two thirds of the pension the member would have received at normal retirement date.

For Money Purchase Schemes the normal death benefit is a refund of the member's accumulated fund. If the scheme is contracted-out, the rules may provide for a pension from the accumulated fund.

Deferred members

For Final Salary Schemes, the normal death benefit is the refund of the member's contributions. If the scheme is contracted-out, the rules may provide for:

- guaranteed Minimum Pension payable to a surviving spouse, or
- up to ⅔ of the member's preserved pension payable to the surviving spouse.

For Money Purchase Schemes, the normal death benefit is a refund of the member's accumulated fund. If the scheme is contracted-out, the rules may provide for a pension from the accumulated fund.

Pensioners

If a pensioner dies within a guarantee period, the remaining unpaid instalments of pension for the guarantee period are paid to the beneficiary, free of tax.

For Final Salary Schemes, the rules of the scheme may allow a pension to the surviving spouse of up to two thirds of the member's pension.

For Money Purchase Schemes, the member decides at the time of retirement what level of pension is payable to a surviving spouse, which can be up to two thirds of the member's pension. The level of this will, of course, affect the amount of pension received by the member.

The scheme rules may provide for conditional payments to widows or widowers. These conditions could be things such as stopping or reducing the pension if the widow or widower remarries, or paying a much lower pension if the widow or widower is considerably younger than the pensioner. The widow's or widower's pension may be increased if there are young dependant children – up to the age of 18, or 21 if in full-time education. Even if the widow or widower dies, the pension can be continued until the children reach these ages if they are still dependant.

Other enhanced benefits

The scheme trustees may enhance the benefits due to any member in excess of their actual entitlement according to the trust document at retirement age. These enhancements are known as discretionary enhancements, and must remain within Inland Revenue maximum limits.

For example, enhanced benefits could include an escalation rate of the pension above the limited price indexation. However, it would still have to be within the 5% maximum limit imposed by the Inland Revenue.

The employer may also request the trustees to enhance a member's benefits on early retirement, redundancy, ill health, or death in service (benefits to a surviving spouse).

Early leavers and transfer options

Leaving Service

What options are open if you leave the employer before pension age?

- You may take early retirement. This is normally available from age 50 onwards, but earlier retirement may be allowed on ill health grounds, or for certain employments.
- If you have had less than two years' pensionable service, you may take a refund of your contributions – but this is subject to a 20% tax charge.
- If you are a member of a Final Salary Scheme, you may preserve your benefits within the scheme. This means that your pension at the normal retirement age will be

calculated according to the years of service at the time you leave.

- If you are a member of a Money Purchase Scheme you may leave your funds fully invested in the scheme. You can then take the benefits at the normal retirement age.
- You may be able to transfer the capital value.

Transfer of Occupational Schemes

Occupational Schemes may be transferred to:

- section 32 policies,
- another employer's occupational scheme,
- Personal Pension Plans, or
- Stakeholder Pensions.

Section 32 Policies

This type of scheme gets its name from Section 32 of the 1981 Finance Act, which enabled these policies.

These policies are designed to take transfers from Occupational Pension Schemes. They may not take transfers from any other type of pension scheme. Once the transfer has been made, no further contributions may be made. The transfers may be made from Occupational Schemes which were contracted out of SERPS via the Guaranteed Minimum Pension (GMP) test. This meant that the Guaranteed Minimum Pension would at least equal the provision of a pension under SERPS.

A Section 32 Policy means that the company taking on the scheme must guarantee to pay at least the GMP at retirement.

Section 32 Policies	Personal Pension Plans or Stakeholder Pensions
Guarantee to pay the GMP at retirement date, with possibility of additional benefits.	No guarantee – the benefits depend on the performance of the investments in the fund.
No additional contributions allowed.	Further contributions allowed – see the limits.
Benefits may be taken between the ages of 50 and 75 without the member retiring – but the funds must be sufficient to provide the GMP from the State Pension age.	Benefits may be taken between the ages of 50 and 75 without the member retiring.
Tax-free lump sum limited by Inland Revenue Rules.	Maximum tax-free lump sum of 25% of the value of the fund. However, it may be lower if it was limited at the time of transfer from the Occupational Scheme.
Inland Revenue rules may limit the pension at retirement.	No limits on the pension at retirement.
Any surplus returned to the employer or retained by the insurer.	There can be no surplus – all the funds are used to provide the benefits.
Any GMP transferred is retained as a GMP.	Any GMP transferred is not guaranteed.
Benefits in respect of contracted-out rights after April 1997 are not guaranteed but may be taken from age 50.	Benefits in respect of contracted-out rights after April 1997 are not guaranteed and are not available until age 60.
Funds may be transferred to Occupational Schemes, Personal Pension Plans, Stakeholder Pensions or another Section 32 Scheme.	Funds may be transferred to Occupational Schemes, Personal Pensions, or Stakeholder Pensions, but not to Section 32 Schemes.

The pension could also be more than the GMP. If the funds exceed the requirement to pay the GMP, the company operating the scheme may use the excess to either:

- pay a tax-free lump sum, or
- buy an additional annuity.

A Section 32 Scheme may also transfer the fund to:

- a Personal Pension Plan, or
- a Stakeholder Pension, or
- an Occupational Scheme.

If you are thinking about transferring an Occupational Scheme, the table overleaf gives a comparison of the options.

Surpluses

The scheme's funds are subject to statutory valuations, which compare the funds held with the scheme's liabilities to present and future pensioners. If there is a surplus of funds, and the surplus is more than 5% of the liabilities, the trustees must provide the Inland Revenue with their plans to reduce the surplus.

In calculating the liabilities, limited price indexation (LPI) may be applied. LPI allows the benefits to pensioners to have a limited increase in benefits each year – the lower of 5%, or the increase in the retail price index (RPI).

Plans to reduce the surplus may include:

- Providing new and improved benefits.

- Contribution holiday for members.
- Contribution reduction for members.
- Refund to the employer. (This refund is subject to a 40% tax charge and must be approved by the Inland Revenue first.)

Legal basis of Occupational Schemes

Occupational Schemes are run by a board of trustees, and overall supervision is exercised by the Occupational Pensions Regulatory Authority (OPRA). The Pensions Act 1995 is the overall governing statutory law.

Trustees

All trustees are subject to regulation by OPRA and, if they are in breach of their duties, OPRA has the power to impose fines of up to £50,000 for each breach. OPRA may also suspend, prohibit or disqualify trustees, and even prosecute if they are found to be guilty of a criminal act.

Members of a scheme have the right to elect one third of the scheme's trustees. However, the following schemes are exempt from this provision:

- Schemes with only one member.
- SSASs.
- Public Sector schemes.

Rules

Schemes may adopt the 'prescribed rules', which are a set of standard rules and procedures for election of trustees.

Alternative rules may be adopted if approved by the members of the scheme.

Investments

There must be a written statement of the scheme's investment policy, unless the scheme's investments are wholly in insurance policies. No more than 5% of the scheme's funds may be invested in the sponsoring employer's business. Trustees are not allowed to make loans from the scheme's funds.

Professional advisors

Professional auditors and actuaries must be appointed by the trustees. These professional advisors must be suitably qualified, and the auditor must not be connected to the scheme (as a member), or to the employer.

Professional advisors have a duty to report to OPRA any failures of the trustees to meet the requirements of the Pensions Act 1995. This is known as whistleblowing, and failure to do this can result in the advisor being reported to his or her professional body.

The scheme actuary must produce a Minimum Funding Requirement (MFR) certificate for Final Salary Schemes. If the scheme is not sufficiently funded, it must make good the shortfall within certain time limits as follows:

- If the scheme is between 90% and 100% funded, the time limit is 10 years.
- If the scheme is less than 90% funded, the time limit is

three years to reach 90%, then a further 10 years to make it up to 100%.

Annual Report

The scheme must produce an annual report, unless it is exempt. Exemptions include:

- Schemes with only one member.
- Public Sector Schemes.
- Unapproved Schemes.
- SSASs.
- Earmarked Schemes.

The report must include the auditor's report, the annual audited accounts, and the latest actuarial valuation certificate.

Executive Pension Plans (EPPs)

In essence, these are Money Purchase Occupational Pension Schemes designed for company directors (who are of course employees) and/or other key personnel. They generally allow much more flexibility, and the employer company may make generous contributions. They are also sometimes referred to as 'Top Hat' schemes.

Great flexibility can be exercised in respect of the contributions to these schemes. Contributions *must* be paid by the employer and additional contributions *may* be made by the employee. The employee contributions can be made by regular payments or by special one-off payments. The tax relief and contribution limits for employees are the same as for ordinary occupational pension schemes.

Advantages

A particular advantage is that the employer can make contributions to this plan, and these contributions save the company the National Insurance liability, currently 12.2%. The combination of tax relief and the relief on National Insurance contributions makes this a very attractive alternative for owner-directors.

If the fund exceeds or looks likely to exceed the normal Inland Revenue limits, contributions may have to be stopped or restricted.

Employer contributions escape any tax liability on either the employer company or the employee. Thus, an employer company can invest profits tax free, and the directors (or other beneficiaries) can receive part of the accumulated fund as a tax-free lump sum when they retire.

The employer may make single contributions to make up for missed contributions in earlier years of service. There is full tax relief up to £500,000 in a tax year. Above this level, tax relief is spread over a number of tax years. Details are the same as those given in Chapter 6, relating to SSASs.

The fact that contributions and benefits such as death benefits and the tax free cash lump sum are related to the salary of the director (or other executive) involved means that this type of plan can be very flexible for a small, director-controlled company. To a large extent, the salary of the controlling director can be set at will. Thus, for example, the maximum tax-free lump sum allowed of 150% of final salary can be determined by voting a high salary. The final salary is actually based on the average of the highest three years' salary within 10 years of actual retirement.

The maximum lump sum can be paid, and it is then valid for only the balance to be used to provide a pension. This provides a way to achieve a large cash sum. The death in service benefits can also be very generous – up to four times salary plus refund of the member's contributions plus interest. This means that, with tax relief on the contributions, it can be a cheap and tax efficient way of providing valuable life assurance.

> **Warning!**
> There is a restriction of the age at which benefits may be drawn from an EPP. The member must be 60 and actually retired from the service of the employer company.

Most major insurance companies have off the shelf packages for EPPs so they can be set up relatively cheaply and quickly. Many companies also limit their charges to 1% (if the invested funds are their own) to compete with Stakeholder Pensions.

Who pays the premium?

Many companies have been formed from businesses previously run by a proprietor as a self employed sole trader, or in partnership. When they were working as self employed, they sensibly started paying premiums to a Personal Pension Plan, or a Stakeholder Scheme. After the change in status of the business to a limited company, they continue paying the premiums privately. At first sight, this seems reasonable, since they continue to get tax relief at their highest marginal rate of tax. The individual pays pension contributions net of basic rate tax (at present 22%), and must claim any additional relief for higher rates. The company, if it pays the contribution, must pay it gross, and claim it as a business expense, against which it gets Corporation Tax relief.

But could there perhaps be any saving if the company made the contribution?

The first thing to do is to look at the rate of Corporation Tax paid by the company. At present rates, this could be 0%, 19%, 23.75%, 30%, or 32.75%. The next thing is to look at the rate of tax paid by the individual. This could be 22% or 40%. By comparing the actual effective rate paid in each case, there could be advantages either way.

Examples

1 XYZ Ltd. Profits £100,000 – pays tax at a top rate of 19%.
   Director Mr. X Earnings £60,000 – pays tax at 40%.
   The director gets more tax relief than the company.

2 ABC Ltd. Profits £50,000 – pays tax at 23.75%.
   Director Mr. A Earnings £25,000 – pays tax at 22%.
   The company gets more tax relief than the director.

However, even this analysis does not take into account the whole cost involved. The director must have the salary to pay the pension contributions. In order to pay the salary from the company to the director there is a National Insurance cost of 23.8% – 11% employee's cost, and 12.8% employer's cost. Furthermore, paying a pension contribution does not reduce the employee's National Insurance liability. Therefore, to calculate the true cost, National Insurance must be taken into account.

Example

Assume a company paying Corporation Tax at 19%, and a director paying tax at 22%, wishing to make a net pension contribution of £2,500.

If the director pays the contribution –

His gross salary must be	£3,731.34	
Tax deducted at 22% £820.89		
National Insurance at 11% £410.45		(A)
Total deductions	£1,231.34	
Net pay	£2,500.00	
Net contribution to Pension Plan	£2,500.00	
Tax relief	£705.13	
Total gross contribution	£3,205.13	(B)
The company pays the director	£3,731.34	
The company pays		
12.8% National Insurance	£477.61	
Total cost to the company	£4,208.95	
Corporation Tax relief on		
this sum at 19%	£799.70	
Net cost to the company after tax	£3,409.25	(C)
The total cost to company		
and director is	£3,819.70	
		(A)+(C)
The total gross contribution		
to the pension plan is	£3,205.13	(B)

If the company pays the contribution:

The cost of the contribution is	£3,205.13	
Corporation Tax relief on this		
sum at 19%	£608.97	
Net cost to the company		
after tax	£2,596.16	
The total gross contribution		
to the pension plan is	£3,205.13	

There could therefore be a considerable saving if the contributions were made by the company instead of by the director. The big difference is, of course, the cost of the National Insurance contributions. However, the calculation must be made according to each individual circumstance. The relative rates of Income Tax paid by the director, and Corporation Tax paid by the company are also a key factor.

In essence this is a 'salary sacrifice' arrangement which benefits from saving the National Insurance cost. Because there is a sacrifice of salary, this will only work in a Money Purchase Scheme, not a Final Salary Scheme. There could also be tax benefits in sacrifice arrangements relating to bonuses or dividends.

CHECKLIST

- Employers with at least five employees must offer at least a Stakeholder Pension Scheme to employees.
- Group Personal Pension Plans and Occupational Schemes are the alternatives.
- There are tax benefits for both employee and employer.
- The scheme must be run by a trust set up for the purpose.
- Inland Revenue limits apply to contributions and benefits.
- Contributions may be made to other schemes concurrently.
- An Executive Pension Plan could be beneficial for owner-directors.

- If the scheme has surpluses, they must be dealt with in defined ways.
- There are various options on leaving service.

Case study

Bernard

Bernard's company has an Occupational Scheme for its twenty employees. He decides to start an Executive Pension Plan (EPP) for himself and his wife, the two directors of the company. The company makes regular contributions each month. Then, at the end of the year, when they might have been considering a bonus, the company makes a special one-off contribution for each of them, and a dividend payment.

This way, they maximise the tax and National Insurance benefit available from contributions to the EPP and from the dividend payments. This also makes use of the flexibility inherent in these methods of payment. The amounts of both dividends and contributions to EPPs can be varied according to the amount of profit made – or even missed if there is insufficient profit.

6
SIPPs and SSASs

QUESTIONS, QUESTIONS

- Are SIPPs and SSASs for experts only?
- What advantage is there in investing my pension fund myself?
- What is the difference between SIPPs and SSASs?

Normally, a pension plan works by members paying contributions to a pension provider, and that provider (usually an insurance or dedicated pension company) invests the money in various forms of investment to provide growth in the fund from which the pension is paid. SSIPs and SSASs provide a way in which the contributor can take some control over the way in which the fund is invested.

These types of schemes provide a useful means of investing a pension fund in a form which could benefit a small business, mainly by the increased range of investments available – often in property of some sort which can be used by the contributor's business.

SIPPs

Normal Personal Pension Plans consist of funds that are invested by the pension provider. These investments include things like equities, bonds, and deposit accounts. The contributor has only limited control over what the fund is invested in.

SIPPs were introduced to allow contributors to Personal Pension Plans to have more control over their own fund's investment. A SIPP is set up under a trust deed. A trustee controls the investment of the fund, under instruction from the contributor. The contributor may be the trustee, but if so, an administrator must be appointed to carry out the investment transactions.

Permitted investments are:

- Stocks and shares traded on recognised Stock Exchanges. This therefore includes equities, bonds and other loan stocks, fixed interest stocks, including preference shares, debentures, warrants, permanent interest bearing shares, and convertible securities.
- Futures and Options relating to securities traded on recognised Stock Exchanges, and relating to currency.
- Shares from:
  – Employee Share Ownership Plans,
  – Approved Profit Sharing Schemes, and
  – Savings Related Share Option Plans.
- Unit Trusts and Investment Trusts.
- Unit linked funds provided by U.K. Life Assurance companies.
- Traded Endowment Policies.
- Deposit Accounts.
- Commercial Property – leasehold or freehold.
- Borrowing in order to finance the purchase or development of Commercial Property. (But there are restrictions

on the borrowing allowed.)
- Ground Rent.
- Individual Pension Accounts (IPAs).

Prohibited Investments are:

- Loans.
- Borrowing for any asset other than commercial property.
- Property may not be purchased from a connected person (i.e. spouse or close relative of the policy holder).
- Property cannot be purchased after the later of:
  – the contributor's 65th birthday, or
  – the contributor's retirement date.
- Residential property.
- Leisure property.
- Land bordering land owned by the contributor.
- Personal chattels, such as paintings, jewellery, antiques, etc.
- Premium Bonds.
- Gold Bullion.
- OFEX shares.
- Shares not listed on a recognised Stock Exchange.

Investing in property

Because the fund can be invested in commercial property, a SIPP is extremely useful for a small business. The proprietor or partner can take out a SIPP, make contributions, and the fund may then invest that money, (borrowing more if necessary) to buy property for the business. The property is then owned by the SIPP and rented out to the business by the pension fund.

This is particularly useful for an expanding business which needs bigger premises. Note, however, that the property must be commercial property, not residential or leisure property, and that it may not be purchased from a connected person. However, commercial property for these purposes does include development property and agricultural property. The rental income, although not taxable in the hands of the SIPP, must be enough to cover interest paid on any borrowings, and any expenses.

Tax benefits

A SIPP represents a particularly tax efficient way of providing a retirement fund from an unincorporated business (i.e. one which is not a limited company). The tax advantages are particularly shown when the fund purchases property for the business.

- The contributor gets tax relief at their highest marginal tax rate on the contributions to the plan.
- The rent paid by the business is a valid deduction from profits for tax purposes.
- The rent received by the fund is not liable to tax.

Borrowing

The fund may borrow money to invest in commercial property if it does not have sufficient funds available. There are, however, restrictions on the amount of money the fund may borrow to invest in commercial property.

The present restriction is that the fund may not borrow more than 75% of the value of the property to be bought.

Example

Property cost	£300,000
Borrowing permitted	£225,000

Therefore, the fund must have at least £75,000 before the purchase can proceed.

The present restriction is in place until 5th April 2006. After that date, the new restriction will be 50% of the existing pension fund. This means in effect that the pension fund must be at least two-thirds of the value of the property.

Example

Property cost	£300,000
Borrowing permitted	£100,000

Therefore, the fund must have at least £200,000 before the purchase can proceed.

Action Pointer

If your SIPP has a property purchase decision to make in the near future, the message is clear – do it before 5 April 2006.

SSASs

The official definition of an SSAS is –

'A scheme with fewer than 12 members where at least one of those members is connected with another member, or with a trustee of the employer in relation to the scheme.'

This means that it is ideal for small private limited companies controlled by members of the same family.

A further definition is given by the Inland Revenue as follows:

'A scheme is defined as self-administered if some or all of the income or other assets are invested otherwise than in insurance policies.'

Small Self Administered Schemes are Occupational Pension Schemes. They must be approved by the Inland Revenue in the same way as any other Occupational Scheme, and benefit from the same tax advantages. Thus, they are subject to the normal limitations on benefits related to earnings at retirement date and number of years' service. For example, the tax free lump sum may be one and a half times the final remuneration in a final salary scheme.

However, they are normally Money Purchase Schemes rather than Final Salary Schemes. It is most suitable for directors because:

• the number of members is limited to 11, and
• the investment risks are higher than other schemes, and
• at least one member must be connected to other members.

In practice, the majority of SSASs have only two or three members.

There may only be one SSAS per company, but a single SSAS may be available for several associated companies.

These schemes are more flexible than ordinary Occupational Pension Schemes, and are very attractive for directors and senior executives. The additional flexibility comes in the form of greater investment opportunities and tax advantages.

Trustees

An SSAS must be set up under an irrevocable trust. There must therefore be trust rules and a trust deed. The number of members must be fewer than 12, and the members are, generally speaking, the trustees of the scheme. If those trustees cannot carry out the day-to-day administration of the scheme, they may appoint an administrator.

A bank account should be set up in the name of the trustees, so that the scheme's assets are shown to be separate from the company's assets.

Pensioneer trustees

One of the trustees must be a 'Pensioneer Trustee' (PT) who is approved by the Inland Revenue. This may be an individual or a company. The PT acts as a 'watchdog' for the Inland Revenue. The Association of Pensioneer Trustees is the official body recognising PTs, and maintains the highest professional standards.

This trustee:

- may not be a member of the scheme,
- must be a signatory of the bank account, and co-owner of the scheme's assets,
- must ensure that the scheme is properly administered,
- must be widely involved with SSASs, and
- must provide an undertaking to the Inland Revenue not to:
  – agree to any action of the other trustees which infringes Inland Revenue requirements, or

– consent to the winding up of the scheme unless approved by the scheme rules.

The PT may not be removed by the other trustees unless there is an immediate replacement, apart from:

- the death of the PT,
- a court order removing the PT,
- disqualification by the OPRA,
- removal of the approval of the Inland Revenue,
- a fraudulent breach of the scheme rules by the PT.

Investment

What makes an SSAS so attractive is the wide power of investment of the scheme funds by the trustees. The investment powers include:

- Commercial property. Property may not be purchased from a scheme member. However, the scheme funds may be used to purchase commercial property to be occupied by the company which is the employer of the scheme members. The scheme could also purchase property from the employer company, to provide a cash injection into the business. A fair market rent must be paid by the company to the scheme for the use of the property.
- Residential property is normally prohibited. However, if it is occupied by an employee as a condition of the employment (such as a caretaker), or by a person in connection with occupation of business premises (such as a flat above a shop), then it may be permitted. (However, this residential property cannot be for the

benefit of a member of the scheme or the member's family.)

- Personal chattels (but the Inland Revenue prohibits the direct investment of a scheme's funds in:
  - antiques
  - rare stamps
  - rare books
  - gem stones
  - fine wines
  - works of art
  - yachts
  - gold bullion
  - Krugerrands
  - furniture
  - jewellery
  - vintage cars
  - oriental rugs).
- Shares in unlisted companies (although the investment of the funds may not exceed 30% of the voting power of any company).
- Deposit accounts.
- Copyrights.
- Financial futures.
- Commodity futures.
- Traded options.
- Loans may be made from the SSAS funds. The lending powers of the funds are as follows:
  - Loans may be made to anyone not a scheme member, and not connected to a scheme member.
  - Loans must not exceed 25% of the scheme's assets in the first two years of its existence (excluding any pension transfers from another scheme), or 50% of the

scheme's assets thereafter. For these purposes, the percentages apply to all assets of the scheme except assets earmarked for a member who has retired or died.
– Loans must be made on true commercial terms (for a fixed term and a commercial rate of interest – defined as bank rate plus 3%). There must be a written loan agreement, and the Pensioneer Trustee must specifically approve all loans.
– If the loan is made to a participating employer, it must be used for *bona fide* commercial purposes.
– Loans must not be made to insolvent companies, or to keep a failing company from insolvency.
– Loans may not be made to a third party resulting directly or indirectly in a member receiving a loan of a similar amount from that third party.

- Loans or investments in a participating employer's business must not exceed 5% of the scheme's assets, unless there is a scheme rule permitting it, and all the members of the scheme agree to it.

It can be seen, therefore, that there is great scope for investment of the pension funds of an SSAS in the business of the employer. This can be by lending money to or investing money in the employer company, or by buying property for the company to occupy.

For small companies, owned and run by the directors, this represents a great opportunity to use these funds in an extremely tax effective way in the business.

- Tax relief is given to members on their contributions to the scheme.

- Tax relief is given to the employer company on their contributions to the scheme (but see restrictions below).
- If any amounts are loaned to the employer's business, that company gets full tax relief on interest paid.
- If the scheme buys property for the company's occupation, that company gets full tax relief on rent paid.
- The scheme funds are exempt from tax on rental income.
- The scheme funds are exempt from tax on any income except dividend income (therefore investing in ordinary shares of the company does have its limitations).
- The scheme funds are also exempt from Capital Gains Tax on the sale of any assets, including property, owned by the scheme's funds.

Warning
If the scheme purchases property, there are a few negative factors to bear in mind.
1 If the purchase represents a significant proportion of the scheme's funds, there could be a risk of it being difficult to sell that property when funds are needed at the retirement of scheme members. However, this difficulty can be partly offset by the borrowing powers of the scheme (see below).
2 If the purchase is of industrial buildings, the scheme cannot get the Industrial Buildings Tax Allowance which would otherwise be available to the company.
3 The company cannot use the property as security for any other borrowing it may contemplate.

Restrictions on tax relief

In general, contributions to the scheme by the employer company are allowable against tax. However, in cases of larger amounts paid in any one accounting year, the tax relief is restricted.

Firstly, there is a general restriction that contributions to the scheme must be justified by the scheme actuary, and within the maximum funding rules.

There is a special restriction if contributions in any one accounting period are £500,000 or more. In these cases, the Corporation Tax relief is spread over a number of years according to the following table:

Amount of contribution	Spread period
Below £500,000	1 year
Above £500,000 and below £1,000,000	2 years
Above £1,000,000 and below £2,000,000	3 years
Above £2,000,000	4 years

Borrowing

Another advantage of SSASs is that the trustees may borrow money. This can be used:

- to buy a new asset for the scheme (for commercial purposes), or
- to pay out an annuity without having to sell one of the scheme's assets.

The second option could be particularly useful if an investment held by the scheme is at a low valuation, and the timing is not right to sell it.

There are maximum limits to what trustees can borrow. This limit is:

- Three times the employer's and employees' ordinary annual contributions, plus
- 45% of the market value of the scheme's net assets (excluding assets earmarked for a member who has retired or died).

Example

An SSAS scheme has assets valued at £500,000, of which £150,000 is earmarked for a retired member. The ordinary annual contributions are as follows:

Employer	£40,000
Employees	£40,000

The maximum borrowing limit would be:

45% of non-earmarked assets (i.e. £500,000 less £150,000)	£157,500
Three times annual contributions (i.e. £40,000 plus £40,000)	£240,000
Total borrowing powers	£397,500

Borrowings must be reported to the Inland Revenue, unless:

- the term is less than 6 months, and
- the amount borrowed is the lower of £50,000 or 10% of the market value of the scheme's assets.

Actuarial valuation

Even though most SSASs are Money Purchase Schemes, all SSASs must have a triennial valuation carried out by a qualified actuary. This is to ensure that the scheme's assets can meet the liabilities. There is also an issue about over-funding of a scheme. This is because an employer company could put excess money into the scheme, simply in order to avoid or reduce its Corporation Tax liability.

The valuation must be submitted to the Inland Revenue within 12 months of the valuation date.

There must also be an actuarial valuation report submitted with the original approval to the Inland Revenue. This report must detail the members' incomes, ages, and retirement ages. It must also show the maximum funding limits, initial contribution rates, and how the assets are to be invested.

Funding basis

Because of the over-funding problem mentioned above, Inland Revenue rules have been in force since 1996 to govern the way in which employer companies make contributions for members of SSAS schemes.

The employer company may choose to make contributions in one of two ways:

1   a percentage of the current remuneration of the member, or
2   a fixed amount determined by the actuarial valuation.

The method may be chosen individually for each member of the SSAS, so that different members may be on different methods. The method, once chosen, must remain for three years. At the end of the three year period, a new method may be chosen for the next three years.

If the method is of a percentage of the current salary of the member, the following table shows the maximum contributions which may be made:

Age next birthday	Normal retirement age 60	Normal retirement age 65
25	28%	20%
30	35%	25%
35	42%	31%
40	57%	37%
45	86%	51%
50	118%	77%
55	301%	105%
60	n/a	268%

If a fund is over-funded, the Inland Revenue requires action to be taken. This could take the form of:

- suspending all contributions until the fund is in balance, or
- increasing remuneration to members, or
- increasing or adding to benefits to members, or
- adding new members to the SSAS, or
- making a refund to the employer company, which is subject to a 35% tax charge.

Relevant and Non-relevant benefits

This is a key concept for SSASs. The scheme must exist for the purpose of providing relevant benefits for its members – that is to say, the provision of a pension, the associated tax free lump sum, and death benefits.

Any other benefits are described as non-relevant benefits, and these are prohibited. Thus, no investments of the scheme's funds may provide non-relevant benefits to a member (e.g. the occupation of a residential property by a member or a member's family). A similar consideration applies to the application or result of the borrowing powers of the scheme's funds.

In general, an SSAS may provide relevant benefits in more flexible ways than an occupational scheme. This is because the funds are often invested in assets which are not readily realisable (such as property rented to the employer's business). It is common for an SSAS to allow drawdown benefits. As with other drawdown schemes, an annuity must be provided by age 75 at the latest. The trustees must ensure that the market is regularly scanned to determine the best time for annuity purchase.

When a drawdown is being operated, part of the actuary's triennial review must include:

- a check that the drawdown income paid to the beneficiary is within 10% of the market rate for annuities, and
- that the level of drawdown can be maintained by the SSAS assets.

Comparison of SIPPs and SSASs

The table overleaf shows the main differences between SIPPs and SSASs.

	SIPP	SSAS
Structure	Personal Pension Plan	Occupational Pension Scheme
Membership	Individual. However, more plans can be added (e.g. to purchase a property jointly)	Must have fewer than 12 members. Usually one to three controlling directors
Property investment	• Must be commercial property • Can be agricultural or development land • Must not be bought from a connected person	• Commercial property • Can be residential property connected to commercial property • May be bought from a connected person
Borrowing powers	• Up to 5th April 2006 – up to 75% of value of property • From 6th April 2006 – up to 50% of value of fund	• Up to 45% of value of fund's assets, plus • Three times the annual contributions of employer and employee
Trustees	The contributor may be a trustee	There must be a 'Pensioneer Trustee'

CHECKLIST

- **SIPPs:**
  Must be set up by trust deed.
  Wide range of permitted investments, including commercial property.
  Borrowing is allowed.
  There are however prohibited investments, including loans.

- **SSASs:**

  Must be set up by trust deed.

  Must have fewer than 12 members.

  One trustee must be a Pensioneer Trustee.

  Wide range of permitted investments, including property, and loans.

  Borrowing is allowed.

  Funding limits must be observed.

  Actuarial valuations needed.

Case study

Arthur and Annabelle

Arthur's manufacturing company is successfully expanding and he has been contributing pension contributions to an SSAS, together with his wife, the other main shareholder and director. The other members of the SSAS are their financial director and the factory manager.

A new contract means that the business could expand, but needs new premises and machinery. The SSAS fund is able to borrow enough money to purchase the premises together with some of the uninvested funds of the SSAS. The existing premises are sold by the company, and the proceeds used to provide new equipment and machinery needed for the expansion. The business pays rent to the SSAS fund at a commercial rate, getting tax relief, while the rental income is exempt from tax in the SSAS fund.

The business is thus helped to expand and progress, while the retirement fund continues to grow satisfactorily in the SSAS, securing the future for Arthur and Annabelle, and their two key employees.

7
Other methods and problems

- What does 'contracting out' mean?
- Are my Retirement Annuity Policies still valid?
- Is it just as good to save my money in ISAs as pensions?
- Can I make my own provision for retirement without any tax relief?
- What options are open for early retirement?
- What happens to my pension rights if I divorce?

Contracting out

The State Earnings Related Pension Scheme (SERPS) and State Second Pension (S2P) included provisions allowing members to contract out. That means that they may take the additional contributions which would have gone to SERPS or S2P and invest them instead into an appropriate Personal Pension Plan or an Employer's Scheme – which could be a Money Purchase Scheme or a Final Salary Scheme.

The employer and the employee pay lower National

Insurance contributions, but the amount by which their contributions decrease goes instead into the contracted out scheme.

Contracted Out Final Salary Schemes (COFSS)

To contract out via this route, the member has to be a member of an employer's Final Salary Scheme. The contributions to COFSS built up an entitlement to Guaranteed Minimum Pension (GMP) which was broadly the same as the SERPS entitlement on the same contributions. This was available from 1978 to 1997.

This arrangement continued until 1997. From that date, the scheme must demonstrate that its benefits satisfy a quality comparison, showing that they are at least equal to, or better than, a series of test benefits known as the Notional Reference Scheme (NRS). The NRS provides for benefits roughly equal to S2P. To demonstrate that this is so, the scheme actuary must provide a certificate at least once every three years that the conditions have been met.

Contracted Out Money Purchase Schemes (COMPS)

From 1988, employers could contract out of SERPS (and later S2P) through a Money Purchase Scheme. The money saved from reduced National Insurance Contributions (from both employer and employee) must be paid into the scheme. In addition, the Inland Revenue makes a contribution once a year. The amount of this additional contribution depends on the age of the employee, and increases as the employee gets older. This is known as the Age Related Rebate.

These contributions are kept separate from any other contributions, and they are known as protected rights. Benefits under protected rights may be taken from age 60, and are governed by the normal rules relating to State Pensions. In particular, these protected rights may not be used to provide any lump sum on retirement. They must be used entirely to provide a pension.

Contracted Out Individual Pension Schemes (COIPS)

Since 1988 employees who were not contracted out through an employer's scheme were entitled to contract out through an Appropriate Personal Pension (APP). This is now available as:

- Personal Pension Plan.
- Stakeholder Pension.
- Free Standing Additional Voluntary Contribution.

The principles governing these contributions are similar to those outlined above for COMPS. In particular, the contributions are treated as protected rights. However, the main difference is in the method of contributing. The employer and the employee continue to pay the full National Insurance contributions, and at the end of the year, the Inland Revenue make a rebate to the provider of the APP.

Retirement Annuity Plans

These plans were the precursors of Personal Pension Plans. Since 30 June 1988, new plans are no longer available, but plans taken out are still valid, and governed by the rules governing them when they were taken out.

Contributions and tax relief

Contributions were only allowed to people having income from:

- employment,
- self-employment, or
- furnished holiday lettings.

The maximum limits are slightly different from those under Personal Pension Plans, as follows:

Age at start of tax year	Maximum percentage of earnings
Up to 50	17.5%
51 – 55	20%
56 – 60	22.5%
61 – 74	27.5%

Contributions are not subject to the earnings cap, as are Personal Pension Plan contributions.

If there is a difference between the limits under Personal Pension Plans and Retirement Annuity Plans, and the individual pays contributions under both types of plan, then the limit which may be paid into Personal Pension Plans is governed by the following table:

Age at start of tax year	Maximum percentage difference between RAPs and PPPs
35 or less	Nil
36 – 45	2.5%
46 – 50	7.5%
51 – 55	10%
56 – 60	12.5%
61 – 74	12.5%

Tax free lump sum

The Retirement Annuity Plan fund may be used to provide a tax-free lump sum, in the same way as Personal Pension Plans. However, there is a different limit. The limit is calculated at three times the value of the residual pension left after the lump sum is taken. For plans taken out after 17 March 1987, the lump sum was limited to £150,000 for each policy.

Saving schemes and ISAs

The majority of the pension planning vehicles considered in this book are specialised ones, with tax or other advantages. In return for these advantages, the benefits are restricted in certain ways. However, it is always possible to make use of regular savings methods to build up a fund which can be used for retirement benefits.

Using regular savings in this way does not attract any special tax advantages, unless the savings are in the form of an ISA, or any other tax sheltered form. There is equally no restriction on the way these funds may be used. That may represent a great flexibility, but it may also be a disadvantage. For instance, if you wanted to retire before age 50, any savings scheme could be used to fund that purpose. The disadvantage is that the funds are not tied up until your retirement age, and you may draw on them at any time for other purposes. They are not then available when needed for retirement. Self-discipline is therefore needed.

The main principles of saving and investing are considered in more detail in Chapter 9, and Appendices 3, 4 and 5.

ISA or pension?

With tax relief available to a certain extent on both ISAs and pension contributions, it is worth comparing the relative advantages and disadvantages of each. These are compared in the following table:

Feature	ISA	Pension
Tax breaks on income	Free of income tax on interest but not dividends	Free of income tax on interest but not dividends
Tax breaks on contributions	None	Full tax relief at highest rate of tax
Access to the money	Fully accessible at any time	Tied up until retirement age – earliest normally 50
Restrictions on contributions	£5,000 per year per individual	Age related percentage of earnings, but £3,600 (gross) may be contributed regardless of earnings
Guarantees	None – the income is dependent on interest rates or investment performance	Annuity is guaranteed and can have built in increases each year
Flexibility	Totally flexible – capital can be accessed at any time	The capital is gone once the annuity starts
Risk spreading	Risk can be spread by wide selection of assets	Risk can be spread by wide selection of assets within guidelines – but certain types also offer increased possibilities of investment

The comparison shows several interesting features:

- A younger person may be able to take more advantage of ISAs, since the limit may be more than their earnings limit.
- A higher rate taxpayer may benefit from a large tax benefit when paying in, but then is often only a basic rate taxpayer when receiving the annuity.
- An ISA demands more self-discipline to retain the investment and not draw on it.
- Both types of investment allow a fairly wide investment choice.
- Of course, both ISAs and pension contributions may be made concurrently, benefitting from the advantages of each.

An interesting comparison can be made of the projections for saving in an ISA and in a Pension Plan, then taking the benefits. Assuming a growth rate in the fund of 5%, the funds accumulated from an investment of £100 per month from age 30 to age 60 would be as follows:

- An ISA fund of just over £81,500.
- If this fund were used to produce an income, the ISA fund invested in fixed interest investments could, at rates current when writing this, achieve a return of 6%, which gives a tax free income of just over £4,890 a year.

Investing £100 per month net in a pension plan means that the grossed up contribution for a basic rate taxpayer is £128.21, which would produce a fund of just over £104,500.

- If this fund were used to provide a level annuity for a

male non-smoker, non-guaranteed, the annuity rate current at the time of writing this would be 6.42% gross – and it would be liable to tax. Therefore, if the person was a basic rate taxpayer in retirement, the net amount of the annuity would be nearly £5,240 a year, but a higher rate (in retirement) taxpayer's net annuity would only be just under £4,025 a year.

Investing £100 per month net in a pension plan means that the grossed up contribution for a higher rate taxpayer is £151.28, which would produce a fund of just over £123,350.

- If this fund were used to provide a level annuity for a male non-smoker, non-guaranteed, the annuity rate current at the time of writing this would be 6.42% gross – i.e. it would be liable to tax. Therefore, if the person was a basic rate taxpayer in retirement, the net amount of the annuity would be nearly £6,180 a year, but a higher rate taxpayer's net annuity would only be just under £4,750 a year – still less than the tax free income of the ISA investment.

However, if the investments continued to be made until age 65, the picture looks quite different as follows (all other assumptions the same as above):

- The ISA fund would be just under £110,850. This would produce a tax free income at 6% of just over £6,650.
- The pension plan contributions for a basic rate taxpayer would produce a fund of just over £142,115. The annuity produced by this for a 65 year old would be 7.4% gross, and for a basic rate taxpayer in retirement,

this would mean a net annuity of just over £8,200 a year, or for a higher rate taxpayer in retirement, just under £6,310 a year.

• A higher rate taxpayer's fund would amount to just under £167,690 at age 65. The net annuity produced by this would be just over £9,675 for a basic rate taxpayer in retirement, and just over £7,445 for a higher rate taxpayer in retirement.

Thus, it can be seen that the relative advantage of pension contributions gets more as the age of retirement advances, and less as the retirement age is lower.

FURBS (Funded Unapproved Retirement Benefit Scheme)

Why should anybody want to use an unapproved scheme?

We have seen that certain Inland Revenue restrictions apply to approved schemes, in return for the tax relief and concessions. Amongst other things, these restrictions include:

• Maximum pension limit of two thirds of final salary.
• Earnings cap applied to the proportion of earnings which may be contributed.

An unapproved scheme can be used when the Inland Revenue restrictions penalise higher earners, particularly directors. Because the scheme is unapproved, it can increase the retirement benefits above the Inland Revenue limits. However, because the scheme is unapproved, there is no tax relief on employees' contributions, and the scheme's fund is not tax sheltered. However, a company employer making contributions to a FURBS is allowed this amount as a deductible item for tax purposes. (But the employee for whose benefit the contribution is made is taxed on this amount as a benefit in kind, and is therefore liable to Income Tax and National Insurance contributions on it).

A FURBS is a single member scheme, set up under a trust document. Contributions may be made by the employee and the employer company.

The advantages of a FURBS are:

- There is no requirement to use the fund to purchase an annuity.
- The entire fund could be used to pay a tax free lump sum.
- There are no limits on benefits payable.
- There are no restrictions on the investment powers of the trustees.
- The requirements of the Pensions Act 1995 do not apply (i.e. there is:
  – no minimum funding requirement,
  – no need to appoint member-nominated trustees,
  – no need for a scheme auditor or actuary,
  – no need for audited accounts,
  – no disclosure of information requirement).
- There is no age limit on taking any benefits.

UURBS (Unfunded Unapproved Retirement Benefit Scheme)

There are no contributions to the scheme, and therefore no tax liabilities. The employer company merely makes a promise to the employee of the benefits payable at retirement – either in the form of pension paid, or lump sum.

When the benefits are paid, they are fully taxable on the employee and fully allowable as an expense of the employer company.

Early retirement

Rules for schemes vary considerably for early retirement.

Occupational Schemes

Each scheme has its own rules relating to early retirement, but they must be within the framework of the Inland Revenue permitted rules. The Inland Revenue rules allow retirement at any time from age 50. The scheme rules may allow early retirement at any age provided it is not lower than 50.

An Occupational Scheme should provide that in order to retire early, the member must actually leave the employment. Other rules commonly included in Occupational Schemes include:

- Early retirement must be subject to the consent of the employer. You should not assume that this will be granted automatically.
- Preferential terms for those who retire directly from the employer's service (as opposed to those who retire after having left the employer's service).
- There may be enhanced pension rights for early retirement if offered as part of a redundancy deal.

The pension rate will of course be much lower because of two factors:

1   The benefits will have been paid for a shorter period.
2   The life expectancy will be much higher.

The new lower rate may be defined by the scheme rules, or by recommendation from the scheme's actuary.

If the scheme includes contracted-out contributions, there may be additional problems. As we have seen earlier in this chapter, contracted-out contributions are known as 'protected rights' contributions. This means that the pension will not normally be payable until age 60, and that the pension must be at least the 'Guaranteed Minimum Pension' (GMP). This means the same amount as would have been provided by SERPS or S2P for the same contributions. Thus, early retirement would not be permitted in relation to the contracted-out contributions until age 60. In addition, the reduction in pension may well reduce it to an amount less than the GMP. Thus, schemes which include contracted-out contributions may not permit early retirement until the reduced pension is at least equal to the GMP.

Additional Voluntary Contributions (AVCs) and Free Standing AVCs (FSAVCs)

Although AVCs are considered as part of the main Occupational Scheme, the Inland Revenue rules allow different retirement rules to apply for that part of the funds represented by AVCs and FSAVCs. These rules allow retirement any time between the ages of 50 and 75. However:

- The AVC pension may be taken without having to retire from the employer's service.
- The AVC pension does not have to be taken at the same time as other benefits.
- These provisions only apply if the trustees of the scheme permit. They are not automatic rights.

Personal Pension Plans

Normal rules allow retirement at any age from 50 onwards. However, there are earlier limits for those engaged in certain professions, such as:

- sportsmen or sportswomen,
- dancers,
- models.

Early retirement due to ill health or incapacity

Occupational Schemes can adopt rules allowing members to take early retirement for incapacity. The pension payable may be reduced, or equal to the pension at normal retirement age. It may even be greater than the pension at normal retirement age – it all depends on the scheme rules.

The definition of incapacity will vary according to the scheme rules, but generally it means that the member is unable to carry on their occupation due to mental or physical illness. Some schemes may include a definition which means that the member is not just incapable of doing his or her occupation, but any occupation at all.

Case law has decided that to be eligible, any medical condition must be permanent – that is, it must be likely to last until death, or at least the normal retirement age.

The area of early retirement through ill health has recently caused more disputes between members and trustees, and many schemes are tightening up their procedures since this area is incurring greater costs for the scheme, and thereby restricting funds available to other scheme members.

Hitting problems

Divorce and pension rights
When a marriage breaks down, and one partner was a member of a pension scheme, the former spouse loses retirement benefits. This includes the death in service benefits and the benefits at retirement age – the pension and the tax free lump sum. The Pensions Act 1995 and the Welfare Reform and Pensions Act 1999 determine how pensions are dealt with on divorce. Pension rights are often the second largest asset after the family home, so they always loom large in settlements. It is not always the case that all assets (including the pension rights) should be split equally on a divorce.

Therefore, it is important to arrive at a valuation of the pension rights of the scheme for an equitable settlement on divorce. The child carer (usually but not always the wife) will probably have little prospect of being able to build up a pension fund of his or her own. The main earner (usually but not always the husband) will have the prospect of continued earnings from which to build up a pension fund.

Courts tend to take one of three main ways of sharing pension value on divorce:

1   **Offsetting**. Taking into account the needs of the children, if any, the court may well award the home to one partner – the child carer. This usually involves a large amount of equity, and instead of splitting the pension, the value of the pension may be offset against the value of the home. For example, the wife may be awarded the house, while the husband may retain his pension rights – and other assets may be used to provide a balancing amount.

2   **Earmarking**. The courts have the power under the Pensions Act 1995 to 'earmark' a portion of the pension rights, including lump sums as well as pension, to the other partner. This method is not usually favoured if the parties to the divorce wish a 'clean break'. It also means that the non-member has to wait until the member's actual retirement before getting their share of the benefits. This also means that the scheme member could cease contributions to the scheme which is the subject of the earmarking order and start contributions to another scheme after the divorce. This would effectively deprive the non-member of part of a larger pension.

3   **Sharing**. The Welfare Reform and Pensions Act 1999 introduced the option of sharing pension benefits. This is different from earmarking in that the pension provider is ordered to split the pension between husband and wife. Each can then make their own arrangements within the rules of the pension scheme. Thus, the non-member need not wait until the member spouse takes their pension benefits. The non-member actually

receives their share by what is known as a pension credit, and this can be transferred externally to another pension provider if desired.

The sharing is done at a fixed date, and thus the non-member spouse will not benefit from any further contributions to the plan made by the member spouse. The exact proportion of sharing between the parties to the divorce will be determined by the court, or by agreement between the parties involved.

All types of pension arrangements can be split on divorce, even including the basic State Pension and the State Earnings Related Pension Scheme (SERPS). A Defined Contribution Scheme (also known as a Money Purchase Scheme) is usually the easiest type to divide between the parties to a divorce, and a Defined Benefit Scheme (also known as Final Salary Scheme) is usually the most complex.

Defined Benefit Schemes

These are the most complex because the benefits at the normal pension age depend on the number of years' service and the final salary of the member at retirement age. There is no fund value to use as a basis. The scheme must be valued as a whole by an actuary, and the benefits due to each member of the scheme evaluated, to determine if the scheme as a whole has sufficient funds to pay its obligations now and in the future. Therefore, assumptions have to be made about several factors, such as:

- inflation,
- investment return,
- growth of earnings generally,

- discretionary benefits to members,
- future salary increases to members,
- career progression of members,
- mortality rates,
- cash flow considerations – i.e. when the money will be needed for benefits.

There is also a minimum funding requirement, to ensure that Defined Benefit Schemes are neither underfunded nor have excessive surpluses. It can easily be seen, therefore, that the valuation of any one member's pension rights in a Defined Benefit Scheme is no simple matter.

However, the court starts from a Cash Equivalent Transfer Value (CETV), which the scheme provider must produce. This figure is based on the assumption that the member leaves the scheme on the date of the valuation. This assumption is nearly always incorrect, and the member's pension rights are greatly undervalued by the CETV method. In these cases, the court will usually appoint a pensions expert to determine an adjusted CETV which reflects the individual circumstances of the case – i.e. the career progression of the scheme member, and the probable date of retirement. The specific needs of both parties to the divorce are taken into account as far as practicable in this process, which is referred to as a pension audit, which takes into account all the pension arrangements entered into by the parties to the divorce.

Defined Contribution Schemes

A great number of schemes come under this heading, including:

- For individuals:
  - Personal Pension Schemes,
  - Retirement Annuity Plans,
  - Stakeholder Pensions.

- For employees:
  - Group Personal Pensions,
  - Group Stakeholder Plans,
  - Occupational Money Purchase Schemes,
  - Additional Voluntary Contributions (AVCs).

In these cases, the fund will be the basis for the CETV. The only case where there may be some difference between the fund value and the CETV is in an Occupational Money Purchase Scheme, where there could be additional death in service benefits provided by the employer to scheme members. In this case, the court would decide whether the cost of a pension audit would justify the possible added value to the non-member spouse involved in the divorce.

State Pensions

The basic State Pension cannot be subject to a pension sharing order by the court. The other spouse involved would have to apply directly to the Benefits Agency to adjust the member's basic State Pension and any other benefits at pension age. Any reduction would then mean that the amount by which the pension was reduced would be paid to the spouse who applied.

SERPS may be made the subject of a sharing order by the court. The SERPS benefits may have been built up in the

SERPS fund, or by contracting out. Any rights which are shared in this way become safeguarded rights for the other spouse, and subject to the normal conditions as any other State Pensions on retirement age.

CHECKLIST

- You may contract out of the State Second Pension Scheme.
- Retirement Annuity Policies are still valid. They have slightly different rules from Personal Pension Policies.
- You may make savings for retirement through various savings schemes, and unapproved pension plans – but there is no tax relief, apart from the general ISA tax benefits.
- Various options are available for early retirement.
- On divorce, the court may make different arrangements for pension rights, depending on other assets.

Case studies

Geraldine

Geraldine starts saving at a relatively early age – in fact, as soon as she leaves university. She puts her money into ISAs, plumping for a simple fixed interest saving ISA. As she progresses in her career, she continues to save in ISAs, eventually putting the maximum into an ISA each year. However, as her earnings grow, she also puts money into her employer's pension scheme, putting additional contributions into an AVC.

In her mid forties, she launches out into self employment, and leaves her ex-employer's scheme fund intact. She starts to contribute to a personal pension plan. Her self employment flour-ishes, and she can make substantial contributions. Taking advice, she invests in a SIPP.

By the time she retires in her mid-fifties, she has funds available from several different sources, and she owns a house with no mortgage. She decides to take professional advice from an independent financial adviser, and is able to tailor her retirement funds for her lifestyle.

Albert
Albert has been successful, and by his late forties he has built up a good professional reputation, and a large pension fund. However, his marriage hits a rocky patch and he and his wife agree to divorce on amicable terms.

Between them, they agree that, as their house is valued at approximately the same as Albert's pension fund, his wife will take the house, while he retains the pension fund. The difference in the values is adjusted by cash from their joint savings and investments. His wife sells the house, it being too big for her, and buys another smaller house, using the surplus cash to produce an income. Albert has to take out a mortgage, for a relatively small house suitable for his needs. He can keep up the mortgage repayments until he retires about ten years later, when he pays off the mortgage from the tax free lump sum on his pension. He still has a part of the lump sum left, and a decent pension adequate for his needs.

8
Retiring and selling your business

QUESTIONS, QUESTIONS

- When should I start planning the sale of my business?
- What taxes are payable on the sale of a business?
- How can I best pass on the business to my children?

Selling your business

Providing a pension is only one aspect of this stage of your business career. The other aspect, which may have more personal implications, is the actual process of retiring. You may have mixed feelings about selling the business and retiring. Indeed some people find that they cannot face retiring, and so just go on, until they die 'in harness'.

But most people want to enjoy a rewarding retirement. Once you have built up your business, you have a valuable asset which you can sell. It is often true that the goodwill of the business rests with you personally. You have built it up over a number of years. The contacts you have made with your suppliers, competitors, and most of all, your customers, make it very personal. Despite all that, people realise that you have to retire, and most will go with your business successor.

Planning ahead

It is always good to plan as far ahead as you can. Make plans for selling the business at least ten years ahead. Decide whether you want to phase in your retirement, or make a clean break.

Very often, you may have a good idea of who you would like to take on the business when you retire. It may well be a member of your family – perhaps the next generation. It may be someone who has worked for you – you may even have trained the person to do the job.

Planning in advance gives you and your successor the chance to smooth out the problems that might otherwise arise. Working with the person who is taking over means that you are able to show them all the aspects of the job – the administration, and book keeping as well as the technical side. You are also able to make sure they build up a good relationship with customers and suppliers.

Handling the negotiations

Even if you have known and worked with your successor for a long time, you must handle the negotiations for sale in a business-like manner. Get a solicitor to draw up the agreement for sale, and suggest that the other party gets an independent solicitor.

You will have to negotiate a price for the business, how it is be paid, what is included in the sale and what is not, and the terms of the hand-over. It is quite usual to have a clause restricting the seller of the business from setting up in competition within a certain time period and within a certain geographical area around the business, (say, a five mile radius).

You will also have to be prepared to supply information, such as the business accounts for the last five years.

Advertising the business

It may be that you do not have a buyer ready to take over your business. If so, you will have to advertise it for sale. Some estate agents deal with business sales as well as property sales. There are also specialist business transfer agents who deal only in business sales. They will, of course, take a commission, but they can often get a better price, and have access to a larger base of people looking to buy businesses. They will have specialist knowledge of the issues involved in selling a business.

Paying tax on the business sale

The sale of a business is a disposal of an asset for the purposes of capital gains tax. Retirement relief was replaced by taper relief. This works by reducing the gain liable to tax by reference to the amount of time the asset has been held since 5 April 1998.The taper is more generous for business assets than for personal assets. The maximum time for taper relief is ten years (for personal assets) or two years (for business assets). The table below shows how this relief works for business assets.

Number of whole years asset is held	Percentage of gain chargeable to tax
Less than 1	100%
1	50%
2	25%

Thus, the tapering relief can never cover the whole of the gain – the most it will reduce it by is 75%.

My book *Small Business Tax Guide* (How To Books Ltd.) gives more details on this and other aspects of business tax.

Passing on the business to your family

You might want to pass on the business to the next generation of your family. The best advice is to start preparing for this as soon as possible. First of all, make sure that the next generation actually want to take on the business. There have been many family arguments caused by a parent's incorrect assumption that a child will want to take over the business.

If the child does want to take over the business, they should do all the training they can, and you should support them in it. It may mean some kind of vocational training, or university course. This could take them out of the business for several years. Be prepared for that.

Creating a partnership

One way of preparing the ground is to bring your child into partnership with you at a point when you feel they are ready for it. Their share of the profit can be determined, giving them an incentive to work for the benefit of the partnership business which will one day be theirs. That way, they learn the responsibilities of self employment, and you can eventually pull out without too much disruption. It also makes a phased retirement easier. You can gradually reduce your involvement in the business, while also reducing your share of the profit.

There still remains the financial settlement, and you will no doubt have some capital in the business which your successor must make provision for paying out to you. It is still a good idea to have a solicitor to look at any agreements made, including drawing up the actual partnership agreement.

Limited Company format

Another way of preparing for business succession is by forming a limited company. The key element in this format is that the ownership of the business is vested in the shareholders. Thus, a typical small family business might start with husband and wife as shareholders. Then, later, as the next generation of the family starts to become involved in the business, shares might be issued to them. The parents, however, still retain control.

Control of a limited company

Control of a limited company is a matter of simple numbers. The shares which have voting rights hold the control of the company. Thus, if one person has 51% of the shares with voting rights, that person has control of the company. It is therefore typical of a simple husband and wife limited company that one spouse holds 51% of the shares, and the other spouse holds 49%. However, when shares start to be issued to the next generation, the shareholdings are said to be diluted. This can best be explained by an example:

Example 1
ABC Ltd.
Mr. and Mrs. Smith own the ordinary
shares of ABC Ltd. as follows:

Mr. Smith -	5,100 shares
Mrs. Smith -	4,900 shares

The total shares in issue are 10,000 – Mr. Smith has 51% and Mrs. Smith has 49% of the shares of the company.

They now issue shares to their children as follows:

John	1,000 shares
Mary	1,000 shares

The total issued shares of the company are now
12,000 shares. The shares issued are now:

Mr. Smith	5,100	42.5%
Mrs. Smith	4,900	40.9%
John	1,000	8.3%
Mary	1,000	8.3%

Mr. Smith now no longer has control of the company on his own.

Thus, when shares are issued to the next generation, the original shareholders must ensure that they only surrender control when the time is right. This problem of dilution can be solved by:

- Issuing further shares to the original shareholders at the same time as the shares are issued to the next generation to ensure that the original shareholders' control is not diluted, (see example 2 below), or
- The original shareholders selling some of their shares to

the next generation rather than issuing new shares (see example 3 below), or

- Issuing a different class of shares with no voting rights to the next generation (see example 4 below).

Example 2

ABC Ltd. – same facts as above:

At the same time as issuing the shares to John and Mary, further shares are issued as follows:

Mr. Smith — 2,000 shares

The total issued shares are now 14,000 shares. The shareholdings are as follows:

Mr. Smith	7,100	50.7%
Mrs. Smith	4,900	35%
John	1,000	7.15%
Mary	1,000	7.15%

Mr. Smith still has overall control.

Example 3

ABC Ltd. Instead of issuing new shares to John and Mary, Mrs. Smith sells some of her shares as follows:

To John — 1,000 shares
To Mary — 1,000 shares

The issued capital is still £10,000, and the shareholdings are now as follows:

Mr. Smith	5,100	51%
Mrs. Smith	2,900	29%
John	1,000	10%
Mary	1,000	10%

Mr. Smith still has overall control.

Example 4
ABC Ltd. Instead of issuing new ordinary shares, new class B shares (non-voting) are issued to John and Mary as follows:

John	1,000 B shares
Mary	1,000 B shares

The total issued shares of the company are now 12,000 shares, made up of 10,000 ordinary shares, and 2,000 B shares. The shares issued are now:

	Ordinary shares	Percentage of voting rights
Mr. Smith	5,100	51%
Mrs. Smith	4,900	49%
	B shares	
John	1,000	Nil
Mary	1,000	Nil

Mr. Smith still retains overall control.

Different classes of shares

A further benefit of issuing different classes of shares is that different rates of dividend can be declared on them. Ordinarily, if a dividend is declared on ordinary shares, it would have to be paid on all shares issued. Thus, in examples 2 and 3 above, if dividends are declared on ordinary shares, dividends would have to be paid to all the shareholders, including John and Mary. However, if different share classes are issued, dividends could be declared on the ordinary shares only.

Getting the paperwork right

In order to carry out share transactions, the legal basis of the company – called the Memorandum and Articles of Association – must provide for it.

Authorised capital

The main provisions are to ensure that the authorised capital of the company allows the issue of further shares, and the different classes of shares needed. The definition of the authorised capital of the company is stated in terms of the amount in money and the number and amount of each share. For example, the authorised capital may be expressed as '10,000 ordinary shares of £1 each'. This means that the total nominal capital is £10,000. The nominal amount must always be expressed for all shares.

Issued capital

The shares do not all have to be issued. Thus, of the total share capital of 10,000 shares, there may only be 1,000 shares issued. This means there are a further 9,000 shares which could be issued. Shares do not have to be issued at their nominal value. Private companies often issue shares at a premium. That is, the people buying the shares, pay more than the nominal amount. If, for instance, shares with a nominal value of £1 are issued at £1.50 each, there is a premium of 50p on each share. This premium must be accounted for in special ways, and is only available to the company for certain restricted purposes.

So, if the authorised capital of the company is, say, £10,000, in 10,000 ordinary shares of £1 each, and 9,000 shares are issued, only 1,000 extra shares could be issued. Thus, in example 1 above, if the authorised share capital of ABC Ltd. were £10,000, then Mr. and Mrs. Smith could not issue any further shares. The Memorandum and Articles of Association of the company can be amended, but it is better to have the right provisions in the first place.

The Memorandum and Articles of Association must also provide for shares of different classes, and the rights and duties of those classes must be defined, such as the voting rights, or absence of voting rights, and the rights to dividends. The most common classes of shares are ordinary shares, giving full voting and dividend rights, and preference shares, giving voting rights, but a restricted dividend (usually a fixed dividend). There are also often deferred shares, or B shares, giving limited dividend rights or voting rights. In theory, there is no limit to the number of classes of shares, and the different rights attaching to them.

Phasing retirement

Thus, any combination of share issues can be made, and the shares held by the next generation can be gradually increased as the parents gradually reduce their shareholdings. This provides a way to achieve a phased retirement. The control of the company is gradually handed over to the next generation. The parents can determine the period over which this operates, as long as they have overall control. In the examples above, Mr. Smith is shown to retain overall control by retaining more than 50% of the shares with voting rights. However, it may also be arranged in such a way that, although one spouse does not have overall control, the crucial 50% of shares with voting rights is still held by the husband and wife.

At some point, however, overall control will be handed over.

Phasing can be arranged in this way to coincide with actual working arrangements of the parents. Thus, the phasing of the control of the company by the shareholdings may be the same as the period over which the parents gradually reduce their working hours. On the other hand, the phasing of the working hours does not have to be on the same basis.

Retaining a consultancy

The business does not have to pass to the family, and it may be sold to an outsider, or as we have suggested above, to someone within the existing workforce, who is being groomed for succession. In these circumstances, there is more likely to be a 'clean break'. Rather than phasing out the actual control of the business, it is sold outright.

However, even in these circumstances, it is often a condition of the sale that the previous owner retains a consultancy agreement. This enables him or her to continue to provide advice and assistance over a period of time, often gradually reducing over that period. This provides another way to achieve the phasing in of retirement. It is invariably a help to the new owners, and it also provides an extra income for a short period.

Retaining the business property

We have seen in Chapter 6 how business property can be included in a SIPP or an SSAS. However, business property can be used in a retirement situation to provide an income, even if it is not part of the 'official' pension fund. You could look on the property as at least a part of your pension fund.

In most circumstances, the business rents or owns the property in which it operates. This is true whether the business is in the form of a partnership or a limited company.

However, the property can be owned by the proprietor, or a partner in the business, or a director of the company. The property is then rented to the business. The rent paid is a valid tax deduction by the business, but it is taxable income in the hands of the owner of the property (i.e. the proprietor, partner or director). When the business is sold, under this arrangement, the former owner retains the property, and continues to let it out to the new owner of the business. This provides income during retirement.

In this situation, it is frequently the case that the new owner will want an agreement under which they have the option to buy the property at a specified time in the future. Thus, the income provided by the rent is temporary, but it is replaced by a lump sum realised when the property is sold. However, this will attract Capital Gains Tax.

What this arrangement also provides is some sort of protection against the new business failing. If the new business fails within the period during which it is paying rent, the owner still retains possession of the property, and can either relet it or sell it, as the opportunity arises.

CHECKLIST

1. Start providing for your retirement as early as you can.
2. Plan ahead to sell your business.
3. Think about creating a partnership to ease the transition.
4. Get advice about all aspects of retiring.

Case study

Herbert and Henrietta

Herbert and Henrietta have run a small engineering company – Herbert providing the technical expertise, and Henrietta the administration and book-keeping skills.

As they approach retirement age, they would like to pass on the business to their children – two sons. One son had been interested in engineering, and even worked for his parents after leaving university, but has since moved on to another job. The other son trained as an accountant, and also has a good job. Both sons are married with children of their own.

Herbert and Henrietta call the family together to talk to them about it. The first son initially sounds interested, but his wife later talks him out of it, preferring the security of his present employment with a large firm. The second son is also not interested in taking over the family business. So Henry and Henrietta decide reluctantly that they will have to sell the business. They contact a business agent to advertise the business. There are a few initial enquiries, but none is interested enough to take it any further.

The second son who is an accountant then follows up a business contact who may be interested in taking over the business. After protracted negotiations, Herbert finally agrees a deal to sell the business. However, taking advice from his son and the solicitor dealing with the contract for the sale, he decides to retain ownership of the property in which the business was carried on, letting it to the new owner of the business. The agreement gives the new owner the option to buy the property after five years. However, the new owner does a bad job of managing the business and it fails after three years. Herbert and Henrietta then sell the site to a property developer at a good price. Although they are disappointed that the business no longer continues, they are financially secure, and take professional advice on investing the proceeds to produce an income.

9
Supplementing your income in retirement

Many people have to supplement their income in some way when they retire. You may well have a lump sum which you have either saved or which you got when your pension plan matured. This chapter looks at supplementing your income by savings and investments. If you have no lump sum large enough to invest, you may be able to realise some of the value locked up in your home, and we also look in this chapter at equity release schemes.

General principles of saving and investing

What do you want to do?
If you aim for nothing, you will probably hit it. Many people feel they would like to save or invest, but it remains a vague

feeling. They may succeed in putting aside some money in a savings account of some sort, but it goes no further. They have no purpose or aim in their saving. The savings they have may be a nice little nest egg, but if it has no direct purpose, it can too easily get used up on the first emergency, or even the first whim, that comes along.

Make it your first task to sit down and think about your aims. This will help you to structure your savings and investments. For example, if you want to save for your retirement, you will want to put your savings somewhere you cannot touch them until your retirement date. Otherwise, you might be tempted to use the money for something else, and find yourself short when you come to retire.

Here are some of the most common aims for saving:

- Generating an income.
- Protecting your capital.
- Combating inflation.
- Providing for your retirement.
- Passing on your wealth to the next generation.
- Putting a deposit on a house.
- Paying for education of your children or grandchildren.
- Having the holiday of a lifetime.
- Buying an expensive item such as a boat.
- Replacing a car.

In this chapter, we are thinking mainly about generating an income for your retirement, but you should also be aware of the possible other uses for savings. You may well want to use savings for a holiday, or to replace the car. Then there are also the occasions when some urgent repair may need to be done on the house. It is always wise to bear in mind the effect of inflation, so try to obtain from your savings an income that has at least the possibility of escalating year by year, particularly if you have no other income.

At all times, be aware of your changing circumstances, and plan your savings with them in mind. Changes usually happen slowly, and we do not always recognise them. Therefore, take time every so often – say every five years – to review where your life is and where it is going. Then make any changes necessary to your saving habits.

Keep it flexible

Unless you are endowed with powers of second sight, you do not know what the future holds. One in three marriages end in divorce, and a divorce can seriously upset the best planned savings and investment strategy. Divorce may be the most obvious wild card in the pack, but there are so many other things which can cause your plans to go awry – ill health, for example.

It is always a good idea to try to make your savings as flexible as possible. Ask questions about any investment you undertake, such as:

- Can I unscramble it if necessary?
- Is it readily realisable?
- Is the value liable to fall as well as rise?
- Can I pass it on easily to my descendants?

Evaluating the risk/reward relationship

When making your plans for savings and investments, you must decide about the degree of risk you are happy with. This does not mean that your degree of risk is set in concrete. You may change your attitude to risk at different times of your life, or depending on how much money you have to invest. Remember one of the first principles – review your circumstances regularly (and this includes a changing attitude to risk) and be ready to change your plans if necessary.

Evaluate the risk

There are some obvious pointers to a high-risk investment.

Assessing the quality of information

If you get chatting to a fellow at the pub, who you only know by sight, and he recommends a sure-fire tip for the 2.30 at Newmarket, you would not put all of your savings on it. If that same fellow offered to sell you some shares in a gold-prospecting company which had just found gold in the wilds of Alaska, your reaction would probably be the same.

Your assessment of the risk is coloured by your judgement of the quality of the information. One of the main factors in this is the trust and confidence you have in the person giving you the information.

TOP TIP

Here is another **Golden Rule of Investing**:
- You cannot have too much information.

But information always comes from someone. It may be the man in the pub, or the pages of the *Financial Times*, or anywhere in between those two extremes.

If you are at all uncertain, try to corroborate the information with someone in whom you have confidence.

What is behind it?

All forms of saving and investment have something behind them. Take, for instance, a Building Society account. By saving in this you are putting money into a large pool which is then loaned to people buying a house. That is very simple to understand, and very 'transparent'. You can easily see that the ultimate investment of the money is in bricks and mortar.

Other forms of investment may not be quite so transparent. A name such as 'General Amalgamated Consolidated Portfolio PLC' does not really give any clue as to what your money would be invested in. So always make a point of trying to find out what is behind it. Is it a chain of seedy night clubs? Is it an international group exploiting the resources of the third world?

The most successful investors have a principle that they only invest in companies that are transparent and easy to understand. Try this as an acid test – can you explain the company and why you are putting your money in it to a ten year old?

Remember – you cannot have too much information.

How big is it?

A further indicator of risk is the size of the company or fund into which you are investing. Taking the example of the Unit Trust, look at the literature. What is the size of the fund? Is it several millions? Or is it tens of millions? Or for a company, what is the total market value of all the shares in issue? (This is known as the market capitalisation).

When you know how big the fund or company is, you can make your own decisions. This is one area where big may be beautiful, but smaller companies or funds often provide better performance.

How Marketable is it?

Another factor in judging the degree of risk attaching to a particular investment is the extent of marketability. The ultimate in marketability for company shares is, of course, the Stock Exchange. In order to qualify to be traded on the Stock Exchange, a company must meet stringent requirements. Anybody owning shares in those companies may sell them openly to any other willing buyer. The number of transactions on the Stock Exchange runs into millions every day.

At the other end on the scale could be a small family company. The shares may be owned by, say, mother, father, and two sons. If one of them wanted to sell their shares, the rules of the company may well say that they may only sell them to directors of the company. Even if this rule did not exist, it would not be easy to find a buyer outside the family willing to buy shares in that company.

In general terms, shares in smaller companies are not so marketable as shares in bigger companies.

Short term or long term?

In judging the degree of risk, you need to think about whether your investment is going to be short term or long term. This will affect your attitude to risk.

If you want to invest long term, you must take into account the effects of inflation. This is obviously not so important for the short term. Thus, if you want to put some money away for a specific purpose, and you know that you will be drawing it out in, say one year's time or less, then a deposit with a bank or building society represents a low risk investment. For the same length of time, investing in shares on the stock market would be a high risk, because you would not be sure that you would not make a loss, especially when dealing costs are taken into account. Share prices can fluctuate, and they may have lost money in the short term, just when you need to take the money out.

If you want to invest long term, and not have to dip into the capital, then a deposit in a bank or building society would be a high risk. It would be virtually certain that the capital invested would be worth less in, say, ten or fifteen years' time than it is now. That is because inflation will have eroded the purchasing power of the money.

Investing in shares for the long term is not so great a risk as for the short term. Historically, prices of shares have at least kept up with inflation. If you seriously believed that inflation would be negative – i.e. deflation – then the above advice would be reversed.

Timing

Timing has an effect on your judgement of risk. This is particularly so when looking at investments with a fixed term. The fact of a fixed term means that the circumstances at the time the investment matures are fixed. It may be that the value you receive at maturity is dependent on circumstances such as the amount of the Stock Exchange Index. Or the circumstances at the time of maturity may not be favourable for re-investing the proceeds.

As a general rule, investments with a fixed term are more risky than open ended ones.

Taking a risk

When you have made your assessment of the risk involved, you can then apply your own principles of how much risk to take when making your investments. If you are happy to take a fairly high risk, at least with some of your money, then you will want to look at the best returns available.

Playing safe

If you decide that some, or all of your money should be in low risk investments and savings, then you will look very carefully at the degree of safety. If there are any guarantees, you will want to find out exactly what is guaranteed. Then, within these guidelines, find the best return you can get for your money.

Specific investments

My book *Managing your Money in Retirement* (How To Books Ltd.) gives more detailed explanations of various forms of investment, and at the end of this book Appendix 3 gives more details about investing in stocks and shares, whilst Appendix 4 gives more details of investing in your country. Appendix 5 gives details of investing in life assurance policies.

Equity release

You may have a large value locked up in your home, but how can you use it for your benefit?

You could sell the house and use the capital to invest and generate income. However, this has the drawback that you need to find somewhere to live when you have sold your house. You could, of course, rent a home. This means, though, that you have to be able to rent a home for less than the income your investment generates, otherwise you would be out of pocket over the deal.

You could also sell the house, buy a cheaper house, and invest the cash left over – this is known as downsizing.

This option could sometimes work if your children have all left home, and you do not need such a big house. However, do not underestimate the costs of buying and selling, moving, and making any necessary improvements to the new house.

The answer could lie in equity release.

> ### Facts and figures
> At the end of March 2004 there were 73,079 equity release mortgages valued at £3.1bn. The elderly are taking advantage of the rise in house prices to unlock equity in their homes. They released more than £1.1 billion last year — an annual rise of 69%.

So what is equity release? It is a way of raising money on the value locked up in your home. It is common for pensioners to be cash poor but property rich. They do not have much disposable cash or income, but they do have a large value in their house. Equity release is a way of accessing that value so that you have some of it in the form of cash which you can use either for income, or to spend.

Equity release is a mortgage loan taken out on the security of the house. This can in some circumstances be done where there is an existing mortgage, but more commonly, it is done where there is no mortgage outstanding on the house. The key feature of an equity release mortgage is that there are no monthly repayments to make. The capital only becomes repayable when you die, or when you and your spouse go into a residential home. Because of this feature, equity release schemes are really only suitable for older people. Currently, the earliest age at which equity release schemes are available is 60. This feature also means that the amount you can borrow is limited, and dependent on your age.

Security

In the past, some equity release schemes were mis-sold. Therefore, all current providers of these plans should be affiliated to SHIP (Safe Home Income Plans). They should all have a negative equity guarantee. That means that they guarantee that when the property finally has to be sold, and the mortgage repaid, the debt will not exceed the proceeds of the property sale.

Steps to take

1   Gather information. There are many providers of equity release mortgages. Search the market. Always use an SHIP registered provider.

2   Talk to an independent financial adviser. They will look at your circumstances, and look at the whole market.

3   Talk about it to your family – that is, the people to whom you are leaving your estate when you die. This, of course, is most usually the children. In practically all cases, they will be in agreement that you should enjoy the benefit of the value in your house, even at the expense of them not inheriting as much as they might have done otherwise. However, it is always best to talk it over with them first.

4   Make your application to the company you (and your financial adviser) have chosen.

The present Home Income Plan market is made up of three main types of plan:

- Shared Appreciation Mortgages,
- Roll-up Loans,

- Home Reversion Schemes.

Shared Appreciation Mortgages

Under this scheme, you take out a mortgage secured on your property. You get a lump sum, and you can do what you like with it. The idea is that you invest this to produce an income. You do not have to pay back any interest or capital, as long as you continue to own and live in the house. When you sell your house, or die, the mortgage loan is repaid, and in addition, a percentage (typically 75%) of any increase in the value of the house since you took the loan is also repaid.

This type of scheme cannot be transferred from one house to another, so the loan must be repaid if you move house. This means that if you want to continue the scheme, a fresh loan application must be made each time you move house, incurring extra costs each time. There is no age limit to this scheme.

Roll-up Loans

Under this scheme, you take out a mortgage secured on your property. You get a lump sum, and you can do with it what you like – again, the idea of this is that you invest it to produce an income. You do not have to make any interest or capital repayments, but the interest is 'rolled up' each year and added to the amount of your loan. The full amount is then repaid when you sell your house or when you die. In times of increasing house values, the increase in the value can keep pace with the increase in the amount of the loan.

Because of the compounding effect of rolling up the interest, you must be very cautious with this type of plan. The interest rates are variable for this type of plan, so that if interest rates increase, the compounding effect gathers pace. This also means that the loan to valuation for this type of plan should be very low – probably no higher than 20% should be considered as safe. A further effect of this is that the longer the plan is likely to be in effect, the greater the risk of running up a large debt. Therefore, you should not consider this type of plan until at least age 70.

If the loan reaches a point where there is a danger of the loan catching up with the property value, you may be asked to start making repayments. It could force you into the position of having to sell the house to repay the loan.

Home Reversion Schemes

Under these schemes, you effectively sell your home, in whole or in part, to the reversion company. You then get either a lump sum or an annuity. You are guaranteed the security of living in the home for the rest of your life, either rent free or for only a nominal sum. Then when you sell your house or die, the reversion company gets the proportion of the sale proceeds. This proportion depends on the proportion you sold the company when you took out the scheme.

The amount of lump sum you would get is never the full market value of the house, because the reversion company has to make provision for you living there for the rest of your lives. Therefore, the older you are, the nearer will be the price you get to the market price.

Questions to ask

Whatever type of plan you are considering, you must stop to consider various things which could become problems. Things to take into account are:

- Are any valuation, survey fees etc. reimbursed by the reversion company?
- Is the scheme transferable if you move house?
- Repairs and insurance – who is responsible?
- Will it affect any Social Security Benefits you receive?
- What do your family think about it?
- What would happen if you took out the scheme as a single person, then married?
- What would happen if you took the scheme out as a married couple, and one of you died?
- What would happen if you took the scheme out as a married couple, and you divorced?
- What would happen if a family member or friend moved in to care for you or provide companionship?
- What is the minimum age?
- What is the maximum loan to valuation?
- What is the minimum property value?
- Is there a minimum or maximum amount you can borrow?
- Is there a penalty for early repayment?
- Is there any restriction on the type of property (e.g. house, flat, maisonette)?

CHECKLIST

- **Savings and Investments**

  Sort out your investment aims and objectives.

  Review them regularly.

  Try to keep your options open.

  Think about the next generation.

  Decide your approach to risk.

  Evaluate the risk factor in any investment.

- **Equity release**

  Release the value locked up in your home.

  Make sure the provider is affiliated to SHIP

  Discuss it with your family.

  Take advice.

Case studies

Brenda

Brenda is still about five years off retirement age, but has just been widowed. She has not worked for many years. Her husband had a good job, and they lived well on his salary. His life was insured, so she has a capital sum. She wants to be able to live as well as she can from investing that capital. She might decide to take some work, but she is not sure yet. She would like to be able to take a little time over this decision. She would like to be able to make the decision to take some work not because it is forced on her by financial pressures, but to help her adjust to life on her own.

Brenda is therefore looking to maximise her income. However, she is still relatively young, and has many years ahead of her. She wants to protect the capital as much as possible, without upsetting the primary aim of generating income.

Charles

Charles is married and has just retired. He has a company pension, and a life assurance endowment policy is due to mature. His wife is a few years younger than him, and she wants to continue working for the time being. Charles does not yet have any positive ideas about what to do with his endowment. He has not yet budgeted for living in retirement, and has a vague idea that with his company pension and the State Pension, he will manage, although he realises that he will not be as well off as before. He always had it in mind that he and his wife would take a cruise when he retired.

A friend takes him aside and tells him he must plan his lifestyle in retirement, and plan his finances as well. He starts to take this seriously, and when the endowment matures, decides to put it for the time being into a Building Society account which gives him good interest, but where he can realise the money without any undue delay.

Another friend then tells him of a sure-fire investment opportunity which involves investing through the stockmarket in the equity shares of the company. He leaves enough money in the account to replace his car when needed, but invests the rest in the shares recommended. For the first year they pay a reasonable dividend, but then their value tumbles. Charles panics, and sells the shares, making an enormous loss. He has learnt the hard way not to put all his eggs in one basket, and to check the quality of information he uses to make investment decisions.

Fred and Freda

Fred has retired at 65, and Freda is 62, but still working part time. She plans to give up work next year. Fred has a small private pension and a State Pension. They would like to add a conservatory to their house, and do some other small improvements. They would also like to have a bit more income to take more holidays and enjoy their retirement more.

Their house is worth £240,000, with no mortgage outstanding. After consultation, they decide they would like to take out an equity release mortgage of £40,000. They have three children, all grown up and married. They call together the children, and tell them of their wish. The children are quite happy that their parents should take out the equity release, so that they can enjoy their retirement more.

When they get the cash from the equity release, they spend £20,000 on the conservatory, and invest the rest, on the advice of their independent financial adviser, to produce a little more income for them. They mentally count their pensions and the little money Freda earns as their day to day living money, and plan to use the income from the investment for holidays etc.

Appendix 1
Pensions simplification
in 2006

At present, there are eight different regimes governing pension savings which benefit from tax relief of some sort. This situation is due to be replaced by a single regime in 2006.

Existing regimes

There is a basic difference between 'defined benefit' schemes and 'defined contribution' schemes, with regard to the level of contributions that may be made, and the benefits available under each type of scheme.

Contributions

- There is an overall 'earnings cap' (£105,600 per year in 2005/2006).
- Occupational Schemes under the 1989 regime allow employees to contribute up to 15% of earnings up to the cap and get tax relief. Employers may contribute up to the earnings cap.
- Personal Pension Plans (1988 regime) – individuals may contribute up to a percentage of their earnings (this percentage varies depending on the individual's age), or £3,600 if that is higher, and get tax relief.

- Retirement annuity contracts pre-dated the personal pension plan regime, but the different rules remain in place. For instance, unused tax relief may be carried back or carried forward from year to year.
- There are different regimes for pre-1970 schemes, post-1970 schemes, and there is also a 1987 regime.

Benefits

- The 1989 regime limits members in occupational schemes to benefits of two-thirds of the final earnings up to the earnings cap, after twenty years' service.
- There are no limits on the benefits from members of personal pension plans.
- There are different rules for the amount of tax-free lump sum payments that schemes may pay.

The new regime

Contributions

The new regime will have two key controls:

1   The lifetime allowance. There will be a single allowance of contributions which benefit from tax relief throughout the lifetime of the individual. This allowance has already been set as follows:

2006	£1,500,000
2007	£1,600,000
2008	£1,650,000
2009	£1,750,000
2010	£1,800,000

Thereafter, the lifetime allowance will be reviewed every five years.

2   The annual allowance. The amount of contributions eligible for tax relief will have an annual limit as follows:

2006	£215,000
2007	£225,000
2008	£235,000
2009	£245,000
2010	£255,000

Contributions will not be limited to a percentage of the earnings cap any more. Contributions will be unlimited up to 100% of earnings (or £3,600 if that is higher).

- If contributions are made in excess of the annual allowance, there will be a charge of 40% on the excess.

Benefits

- All schemes will be able to pay up to 25% of the value of the pension rights (basically this means the pension fund) as a tax free lump sum payment. The maximum permissible such sum will be 25% of the lifetime allowance.
- If the fund exceeds the lifetime allowance, there will be a charge of 25%.
- Funds in excess of the lifetime allowance may be taken as a lump sum, but with a charge of 55%.
- Transitional arrangements will protect pension rights built up before 6 April 2006.

- Primary protection will be given to the value of pension funds in excess of £1,500,000 before 6 April 2006.
- Enhanced protection will be available for individuals ceasing membership of an active pension scheme by 6 April 2006. Provided that they do not resume active membership in any scheme, all of their benefits accruing after 6 April 2006 will be exempt from the charge on the excess over the lifetime allowance.
- The minimum pension age will rise from 50 to 55 by 2010. (But the special arrangements for earlier retirement of people such as dancers and sports people will remain in force.) The maximum pension age will remain at 75.
- Death benefits may be a lump sum, or a pension to dependants, or a combination of both. These benefits will depend on whether the member had started drawing the pension benefits before death, and the age of the individual at death.

Other changes

In addition, the other main changes will be:

- Occupational schemes will have the ability to offer flexible retirement schedules to employees. Thus, employees will be able to start drawing some retirement benefits while still working for the same employer, and thus achieve a phased retirement over a period of a few years.
- There will be wider discretion for investment of pension funds. This will be subject to approval by the Department of Work and Pensions.

- There will be a simplified registration process for pension schemes.
- Non-registered schemes may continue, but without any tax reliefs.

Appendix 2
Inland Revenue requirements for Occupational Pension Schemes

For an Occupational Pension Scheme to benefit from the tax benefits, it must adhere to the Inland Revenue limits defined in the Practice Note IR12. Here is a brief summary of those limits. There are three regimes applying to the limits, with slightly different limits applying to each regime. The regimes are as follows:

- **Regime A** – for members who joined before 17 March 1987.
- **Regime B** – for members of schemes established before 14 March 1989 and who joined between 17 March 1987 and 31 May 1989.
- **Regime C** – for:
  – all members of schemes established on or after 14 March 1989, and
  – members of other schemes who joined on or after 1 June 1989.

Limitations on benefits

Normal retirement pension – maximum of $\frac{1}{60}$ of final remuneration for each year of service up to a maximum of 40 years' service. Therefore the maximum is two thirds (i.e. $\frac{40}{60}$).

This applies to all three regimes.

Earlier retirement

	Proportion of final remuneration	
	Regime A	Regimes B & C
Between 1 & 5 years' service	$\frac{1}{60}$ for each year	$\frac{1}{30}$ of final remuneration for each year of service, with a maximum of $\frac{2}{3}$ after 20 years' service. Earnings cap applies.
6 years' service	$\frac{8}{60}$	
7 years' service	$\frac{16}{60}$	
8 years' service	$\frac{24}{60}$	
9 years' service	$\frac{32}{60}$	
10 years' service and more	$\frac{2}{3}$	

Maximum Lump Sum – maximum of $\frac{3}{80}$ of final remuneration for each year of service up to a maximum of 40 years' service applies to all regimes.

Death benefits

Death in service
The maximum tax free lump sum benefit for a member's death in service is the equivalent of four times the current annual earnings at the time of death.

Death as a pensioner
The maximum pension payable to the dependant(s) of a pensioner member who dies is $\frac{2}{3}$ of the member's pension.

Limited Price Indexation (LPI)

All approved schemes must apply at least a limited price indexation to pensions paid from the retirement date. This means that the pensions must increase each year by the amount determined. This amount is equivalent to the increase in the Retail Price Index (RPI) up to a maximum of 5% per year.

Appendix 3
Investing in stocks and shares

Dealing in stocks and shares

The Stock Exchanges of the world were set up to provide a market place for those wishing to buy or sell shares. The growth of Limited Liability companies produced a need for shareholders to be able to buy or sell shares. Without this facility, far fewer people would have been willing to invest in companies. For the purposes of this book, we are looking at the way the London Stock Exchange works.

To trade in shares, you must deal through a stockbroker. The stockbroker deals on the Stock Exchange through market makers, or through the SETS trading system on the London Stock Exchange.

Market makers

Market makers are traders who deal only with brokers. If a broker approaches a market maker stating that he wants to deal in a certain quantity of a particular share, the market maker will quote two prices – one at which he will offer to buy, the other at which he will offer to sell. The difference between the buying price and the selling price is called the spread. If the broker is satisfied, he will then tell the market maker whether he wants to buy or sell, and the quantity.

SETS

This is a computer system which displays offers for sale and offers for purchase with the quantities on offer for shares. The computer then matches up the buyers and sellers. At the time of writing, this system deals with most of the shares on the 'top 250' index. As experience has shown, any failure in the computer system can sabotage the whole market!

Settling the bills

When a deal has been made, the stockbroker will send you an account. This shows the number of shares dealt, the price of dealing, and any expenses such as stamp duty and their own commission.

Settlement is five working days afterwards. If you have bought, the amount is payable to your stockbroker. If you have sold, the stockbroker will pay you. You may, of course, have sold one shareholding and bought another. In this case, all transactions on the same day will be aggregated and the net amount will be due from you or to you.

Choosing and using a stockbroker

Finding a stockbroker who will take you on as a client is not too difficult. They are in business, and will not turn away the right sort of client. The best introduction to a stockbroker is through a friend or relation who is already a client. They will be able to tell you how good they feel the service is.

Alternatively, a professional advisor such as an accountant or solicitor can probably recommend a stockbroker to you.

Once you have a stockbroker, stay with him or her unless there is some serious problem. The relationship you build up over the years will prove very useful. The service you get from your stockbroker will be:

- advisory,
- execution only, or
- discretionary.

Advisory
This means that the stockbroker advises you either when you request advice on, say, whether to sell, or investing a lump sum, or when he or she feels that a particular purchase or sale would be a good move.

Execution only
This means that the stockbroker will make a certain deal for you, simply on your instructions. They may have no opinion, or they may advise against it, but if you still give the order to go ahead, they carry out your request.

Discretionary
This means that you give the stockbroker the right to manage your shares. The stockbroker will hold your shares in a nominee company, in an account that is designated in your name. They will then go ahead and make any deals which they consider to be right for you.

Having your portfolio managed

A stockbroker will normally take on a portfolio of shares provided that it is of a reasonable size. At present, this would probably mean a minimum of £50,000. He or she would then load the details on the computer, and provide you with a valuation list. This would then be updated and sent to you periodically, typically once or twice a year. A typical valuation statement gives the following information:

- **Summary of Investments by sector**. This shows the total value broken down into the different sectors of the economy.
- **Geographical analysis**. This shows how the investments are spread through the world.
- **Individual details**. This shows each investment separately, and gives the following details:
  – **Holding**. This means the number of shares of each type.
  – **Market price**. This is the price of the share at the date of the valuation.
  – **Market value**. This is the total value of the shares, obtained by multiplying the holding by the market price.
  – **Book Cost**. This is the actual price at which you bought the investment. By comparing this with the market value, you can see whether you are currently showing a profit or a loss.
  – **Dividend rate**. This is the latest declared dividend rate of the company, and is expressed in money terms per share.
  – **Estimated gross income**. This is the dividend rate multiplied by the number of shares. It shows you how

much you should receive in the current year from the investment.

– **Dividend yield**. This is the income expressed as a percentage of the market value. It means that if you bought that investment at the market price on the day of the valuation, the actual income as a percentage of the price is different from the dividend rate. This is called the yield and is the only safe measure of comparing one investment with another.

– **Dividends due**. This tells you when the forthcoming dividends are likely to be paid. There are usually two dividends payments in a year, although some companies pay four dividends in a year.

If you are on an advisory basis, the stockbroker would offer any advice on possible changes at the time of these valuations, or at any time in between.

If you are on a discretionary basis, the stockbroker will carry out transactions on his or her own initiative, and report to you. The effects of these changes will be shown on the periodical valuation.

If you are on an execution only basis, the stockbroker will only carry out transactions when you ask.

Being wary

Some people are wary of giving a stockbroker control of their investments. They may be aware of the security aspect. If a stockbroker holds your portfolio on a discretionary basis, it will be held in a nominee company. There are strict rules governing these nominee companies, and the stockbrokers will have to pay a considerable amount of money as a security bond. This guarantees the investments of the investors.

The other concern some people feel is that stockbrokers may carry out transactions unnecessarily. These transactions, they fear, would not enhance their portfolio, but only generate extra commission for the stockbroker.

This practice is called 'churning'. The allusion is easy to see. The client's portfolio is like milk, being churned to produce butter for the stockbroker. However, this practice is extremely rare, especially amongst reputable brokers. If you suspect a broker of this, you can report it to the regulatory body. If found guilty, the stockbroker faces suspension.

Understanding the index

When we talk of 'The Index', we are talking of one of the indices published by the *Financial Times*. The most commonly quoted is the FTSE 100 share index. This is an index of the prices of the 100 biggest companies quoted on the London Stock Exchange. The change in the index gives a measure of how share prices have moved.

There are however several other important indices, all published by the *Financial Times*. They include the 250 index, the All Share index, the Ordinary Share index, the Non-Financials index, the U.K. Government Securities index, and the FT World index. These measure the price movements of shares in the different sectors.

The movements of these indices are often shown on graphs, with the familiar peaks and troughs. They provide a basis for comparison with the performance of other prices. For example, the price of any one share could be plotted on a graph, and then compared with the FTSE 100 index. This shows whether that share has performed better or worse than the average of the top one hundred. This comparison is often resorted to in considering the performance of unit trusts or investment trusts.

The indices are also sometimes used to show a correlation between share prices and other indicators, such as interest rates.

Reading the prices

Prices of shares are quoted each day in newspapers. The most complete list of prices is in the *Financial Times*. Other broadsheets also quote prices of most shares, and some tabloids also give prices of some of the most commonly traded shares.

The following information can be gleaned from the listings:

- **Notes**. These symbols are explained in the *Financial Times Guide to the London Share Service*. Some notes indicate that the *Financial Times* issues a service on this company. They provide reports on the companies, and free copies of the annual report.
- **Price**. This is the middle price at the close of trading, and given in pence.
- **+ or –**. This shows how the price has moved since the end of the previous day's trading.

- **52 week high/low**. This shows the maximum and minimum prices that the shares have reached in the previous year.
- **Market Capitalisation £m**. This shows the value, in millions of pounds, of the total shares in issue, multiplied by the price. This gives an idea of how big the company is.
- **Yield Gross**. This is the actual return you would receive on your money if you invested in the shares on the day of the report.
- **P/E**. This is the Price/Earnings ratio. It is a key indicator in deciding about investment in a company. The price of the share is expressed in relation to the earnings per share. The earnings per share is the profit of the company as a whole divided by the number of shares in issue.

Picking a winner

Knowing how the stock market works is one thing. What you really need to know however, is which companies to invest in.

Blue Chips

This term relates to the top companies in the country. They are usually the ones in the FTSE 100 index. They represent the companies with the soundest track record, and the strongest financial base. All companies are engaged in a business of some kind, and these are the companies which have soundly based businesses. This is not to say that things could never go wrong. There have been spectacular failures of blue chip companies in the past.

So what factors do you look for in choosing an investment in shares?

Market Sectors

You will see that the share prices quoted are divided into different sectors. These represent the types of businesses. Therefore, if you want to invest in a certain part of the economy (say, banking or leisure), you can see which quoted companies are in that sector.

It is also often more relevant to compare shares in one sector with others in that sector, rather than with other shares in different sectors, or the market as a whole.

Price/earnings ratio

This is the relationship between the price of the share and the earnings of the company (i.e. its profit). For these purposes the earnings of the company as a whole are divided by the number of shares in issue to give the earnings per share.

Example

A company has profits of £3million. It has 10 million shares in issue. Its earnings per share are 30p. If the price quoted for that share is £3, then the price/earnings ratio is ten. This means that the price of the share represents ten years' profit. You would then compare this ratio with the market as a whole, or with the sector in which the company operates.

Quality of earnings

If the price/earnings ratio is based on historic figures, the information is not so relevant as future earnings. Of course, the problem is that future earnings are not a known figure, whereas historic earnings are known.

The price/earnings ratio, in fact, is governed largely by 'market sentiment'. This means what the analysts employed by stockbrokers think of the company. If they have doubts about the future prospects of the company and, in particular, its ability to maintain the profit levels, then the quality of earnings is said to be low.

Dividend yield

This is also a key indicator. It represents the actual rate of return you would get if you invested in the company at the price quoted. The rate of dividend per share is based on an amount per share. The actual rate you would receive depends on the price of the share.

Example

A company declares a dividend of 5p per share, as the only dividend for the year. The nominal value of the share is 25p, so the rate of return would appear to be 20%. However, that is not relevant for these purposes. If the price of the share were £1, then the dividend yield would be 5%, because you would receive 5p income for every £1 you invested.

Earnings Growth

This is a measure of how the company's performance has improved or otherwise. If the earnings per share of a company have shown a steady growth, then the company has obviously improved its performance year on year. If there is a dip for one year in an otherwise steady increase, then there may well be a good reason. If the earnings per share show a steady decline, you would want to find out why before investing in it.

Other markets

The London Stock Exchange is the principal market for dealing in company shares in the U.K. To qualify for inclusion, a company must satisfy certain strict requirements. However, there are other regional markets, and other markets in London. There are the Alternative Investment Market and the Unlisted Securities Market (the A.I.M. and the U.S.M. respectively).

These deal in a smaller number of companies' shares, and the quantity of deals in the shares is much less than in the London Stock Exchange. If you have an investment in a company on the A.I.M., or the U.S.M., therefore, it may not be as easy to sell the shares, simply because there may not be any, or a sufficient number of buyers.

Spreading the risk

TOP TIP

Here is another **Golden Rule of Investing**:
* Do not put all your eggs in one basket.

Collective investments work on the principle of reducing risk by allowing you to invest in many different companies. If you do not have much money, you cannot have a wide variety of shares or other investments.

Collective investments work on the principle of a large number of people investing a relatively small amount, into one 'pot' (which we shall call 'The Fund') and then using that fund to invest in a larger range of investments than each individual could do alone. The risk is spread, and the fund managers are able to manage the fund actively, to achieve the best results.

There are several forms of collective investment. The most common are:

- Unit Trusts,
- Investment Trusts,
- OEICs,
- Investment Clubs.

What is the difference?

Unit Trusts

These are funds which accept money from new investors. The fund is set up as a trust, and trustees have oversight of the fund. Managers do the actual management of the fund. There are over 150 authorised unit trust groups in the U.K. and most of them manage many different funds. So there are thousands of funds to choose from.

The individual funds are usually targeted at particular sectors. For example, there are growth funds, income funds, high income funds, extra high income funds, American funds, blue chip funds, emerging market funds, Pacific funds, and so on. The list is not quite endless, but almost.

Legally, a Unit Trust is governed by a trust deed. This creates a trust between the trustees (i.e. the people who are entrusted to safeguard the money) and the managers. Strictly speaking, the fund is not owned by the investors, but by the trustees for the benefit of the investors.

When a Unit Trust receives new money from an investor, it creates new units in the fund. When an investor wishes to cash in his investment, the Unit Trust pays out the money and cancels the units. This is the main difference between Unit Trusts and Investment Trusts. This feature means that it is an 'open-end fund'.

The price of units in each fund is quoted daily in the financial press and in the financial pages of daily newspapers. The prices are updated daily. The prices are arrived at by totalling the values of all the shares owned by the fund, and dividing that between the number of units in issue. This is another difference between Unit Trusts and Investment Trusts.

Question
What if I have shares, and want to invest instead in Unit Trusts?

Answer
Many unit trusts will accept shares in lieu of payment, provided that the shares are already on their investment list. The shares are taken in by the Unit Trust at their market value, with no deduction for dealing expenses, and an equivalent value of the units is credited to you. This can be an economic way of getting in to Unit Trusts from shares.

Investment Trusts

These are limited liability companies, and are quoted on the Stock Exchange. They have a limited capital, and if you wish to buy shares in an Investment Trust company, you have to buy the shares on the Stock Exchange. This means, in effect, that you are buying the shares from somebody else. This feature means that it is a 'closed-end fund'. It also means that you as a shareholder are the legal owner of a proportion of the company's assets.

The Investment Trust company itself invests in other companies, in much the same way that Unit Trusts do. Usually, however, the Investment Trust Company does not act as an 'umbrella' with several funds. Each Investment Trust company has its own investment strategy, and invests within its plan.

Investment Trusts are quoted companies on the Stock Exchange. The price of the shares is determined in the same way as prices of other shares – that is, by supply and demand. Thus, the total value of their shares can be arrived at by multiplying the price by the total number of shares in issue. This is known as the market capitalisation.

By comparing this with the market value of all the shares which the company owns (its investments), you can arrive at a generally used indicator for Investment Trusts. Shares of Investment Trust companies stand at either a discount to the value of the shares it holds as investments, or at a premium. The amount of this discount or premium is an indicator of market sentiment towards the Investment Trust.

OEICs

This abbreviation stands for 'Open Ended Investment Companies'. As its name suggests, it combines the open-ended nature of Unit Trusts with the company legal structure of Investment Trusts.

A particular feature of OEICs is that prices are given as one price for buyers or sellers. This contrasts to both Unit Trusts and Investment Trusts, where there is a price spread between the price to a buyer and the price to a seller.

Investment Clubs

As the name suggests, this is a more informal type of collective investment. It consists of a number of people getting together (usually on a regular basis) to make their investment plans. Obviously, as the number of people involved is much smaller, there is not so much money to invest, and the members are usually amateurs. However, it does give the members more direct say in the investment of their money. Also, it provides a social occasion.

Because money is involved, it is necessary to have rules and a proper control system to safeguard the money and investments.

The development of the Internet has also seen the emergence of 'investment clubs' on the net. These are more informal, because the club members only exchange information and tips, rather than pooling their money.

Choosing a collective investment

You are now ready to make an investment in a collective fund. What is available to you, and how should you decide? There are many sectors of funds available, but basically, they fall within the following main categories:

- Growth Funds.
- Income Funds.
- High Income Funds.
- Geographical Funds.
- Ethical Funds.
- Split Capital Funds.
- Small Companies Funds.
- Tracker Funds.
- Fund of Funds.
- Gilt and Fixed Interest Funds.
- Tax protected Funds.
- Corporate Bond Funds.

What do they mean?

What is the investment bias or aim of each type of fund? Most of them are fairly obvious from their titles, but here is a brief summary:

Growth Funds

These are slanted towards capital growth rather than income. They therefore provide a lower income than you might otherwise expect, and can be considered a slightly higher risk profile than income funds.

Income Funds

These are geared to produce an income which has a realistic possibility of growing each year to at least keep pace with inflation. The income would normally be expected to approximate to the yield on the shares making up the FTSE 100 index. In practice, many fund managers actually do better than this, and the income is often higher than the FTSE 100 yield. In theory, the capital growth potential should not be so good on these funds, but in practice, historically they have proved to have a good capital growth record.

High Income Funds

These are geared to produce a higher than average income, but this will not have as realistic a chance of increasing each year in line with inflation as pure income funds. The additional income is generated by mixing with ordinary shares, various fixed interest investments in the form of Government stocks, preference shares, debentures, etc. Obviously, the opportunities for capital growth are much more restricted.

Geographical Funds

As the name implies, these funds invest in a particular area of the globe. Typical funds might be 'Far East', 'American', 'Pacific', 'European', 'Eastern European', or 'Emerging Markets'. These funds should be considered as a higher risk, and you should approach them with only as much confidence as you have in the economies of those geographical areas. If you do not know enough, or are not willing to trust an advisor implicitly, you would be better advised to stay away from these funds. Otherwise, any news broadcast could cause you great anxiety, as you see what is happening all over the world.

Ethical Funds

These are funds which either avoid certain negative factors, or which actively invest in certain positive factors. These are funds for true believers.

Split Capital Funds

These are funds in which the units or shares are in two classes – income or capital. One class gets all the capital growth, the other class gets all the income. This obviously gives a higher capital growth to capital shares or units, and higher income to income shares or units than would otherwise be the case.

Small Companies Funds

These may also sometimes be called 'Opportunity Funds'. They invest in smaller companies which the managers believe have good growth opportunities. Again, it is self evident that they are a higher risk investment, but carry the opportunity for high capital growth.

Tracker Funds

These are funds that 'Track' the movement of various Stock market Indices. They do this by investing in the same companies as the companies whose shares are included in the index concerned. Thus, there are funds, for example, tracking the FTSE 100 index, the FTSE All Share index, the Dow Jones index, the Nikkei index, the Hang Seng index, and so on.

These funds therefore do not rely on active trading by the managers, since the investments are relatively stable and unchanging. Investments are only bought or sold when there is any change to the investments included on an index. In the recent past, for instance, when some of the larger building societies demutualised and became companies, they were included on the FTSE 100 index, and tracker fund managers had to adjust their holdings.

Otherwise, there is so little active management that the annual management fee on these funds is usually considerably lower than other types of funds. Many people invest in them for this reason, and because they have little faith in investment managers 'beating' the major indices.

Fund of Funds

These funds invest in other unit trusts or investment trusts. This spreads the investment risk even further, and can be considered an even lower risk investment. However, because of the wide spread of investments, the income performance is not usually spectacularly good.

Gilt and Fixed Interest Funds

These funds, as the name indicates, are invested in Government Securities and other fixed interest stocks. They provide a spread of risk for those who wish to obtain the best fixed interest returns available.

Tax protected Funds

These include Individual Savings Accounts, which provide a

tax free environment for income and capital gains. A maximum of £7,000 per person may be invested in these. Personal Equity Plans were also in this category before they were taken off the market. Investments within Personal Equity Plans may, however, still be traded or switched.

Corporate Bond Funds

These funds are invested in company fixed interest borrowings, such as bonds and debentures. They are most common in Individual Saving Account products. They offer investors a high return tax free income (when in an ISA) but very limited capital growth.

Appendix 4
Investing in your country

'As safe as the Bank of England' is a phrase that denotes absolute security. Certainly there is a place in everybody's savings or investment plans for secure investments backed by the government. These days, there is quite a wide choice, so most people should be able to find something which meets their needs.

Government Stocks

In the same way that companies need to raise money by borrowing from the public, the government also do this. They do this by issuing stocks, most of which have a fixed repayment date, and a fixed rate of interest. This is a really low risk form of investment, and is used by many people for just that feature. For this reason, they are often referred to as 'Gilts'. Many people with a portfolio of other investments also include a proportion of money in Government Stocks.

They are referred to under a series of names, including the following:

- Treasury Stock.
- Exchequer Stock.
- Consols (Short for Consolidated Stock).
- Funding Stock.

- Convertible Stock.
- War Loan.

Whatever name they bear, they are all basically the same – by investing in them, you are lending the government money.

They are also quoted on the Stock Exchange, and for those purposes, they are divided into:

- Short dated (up to five years).
- Medium dated (five to 15 years).
- Long dated (over 15 years).
- Undated.
- Index Linked.

The short, medium, and long dates refer to the redemption date. Undated stocks have no redemption date, and in theory could go on for ever. There are only three of these stocks currently in issue.

The stocks are redeemed at par (apart from the Index Linked stocks). That is to say, the repayment of the amount loaned is made on the stated date, at the same nominal amount at which they were issued. This may not be the same as the amount you paid, since their value fluctuates on the stock market according to the prevailing rates of interest.

Index Linked stocks are ones which have a redemption date, but they are not repaid at par. The amount at which they are repaid is linked to the change in the retail prices index between the issue date and the redemption date.

> **Example**
> If an Index Linked stock was issued when the retail prices index stood at 100, and then repaid when the index stood at 200, the amount repaid would be twice the original nominal amount of the stock.

Because there is this inbuilt gain in the capital (in theory, the index could actually be lower at redemption, but this possibility is so remote as to be out of the reckoning), the interest rate paid on these stocks is relatively low.

Interest

Interest is paid twice yearly on government stocks. It is paid with income tax deducted at source. If you are not liable to tax, you may apply to the Inland Revenue to have the tax refunded.

Buying Government Stocks on the National Savings Register

As an alternative to buying Government Stocks on the Stock Exchange, you may buy them from National Savings. There is a small charge for this, but it is not usually as much as buying them on the Stock Exchange. The other main advantage of buying them this way is that the interest is paid gross – i.e. with no income tax deducted. However, the interest is taxable. This is often the preferred option for those whose income level means that they are not liable to income tax. The vast majority of Government Stocks are on the National Savings Register and available to buy in this way.

Prices of Government Stocks

Government Stocks are quoted on the Stock Exchange, and the price is quoted as a figure for which you may buy or sell £100 worth of the nominal value of the stock. Thus, any particular stock can be priced over 100, in which case it is said to be at a premium, or under 100, which is said to be at a discount. The price is governed by the prevailing interest rates at the time. For example, if prevailing interest rates are around 8%, and the nominal interest rate on a stock is 12%, the demand for that stock is likely to be high, and the price will rise above 100. In fact, in this case, unless the stock had a very short life to redemption, the price would rise to about 150, so that the yield would be roughly equivalent to the prevailing rates.

Yields

The financial press, in quoting prices for Government Stocks, gives yield figures. This means the actual return which you will get on your money and, unless the price is 100, it will be different from the nominal interest rate of the stock. However, there are two yields quoted, an interest yield and a redemption yield.

Interest yield

The interest yield is the actual yield which you would receive on your money if you invested. This is simple to see, as in the example given above. If a stock with a nominal interest rate of 12% is quoted at 150, the interest yield will be 8%.

Redemption yield

The redemption yield is an additional indicator. It can be

calculated because Government Stocks have a fixed redemption date. (Therefore it is not quoted for undated stocks.) It represents the 'real' yield you would get over the remaining life of the stock. In other words, it takes into account the premium or the discount in the price.

I have called this the 'real' yield, because it is important to bear this factor in mind when comparing prices and yields. It is shown at its most extreme in very short dated stocks. For example, in July 1997, the following price appeared in the financial press:

Exchequer 15% 1997 – price 102.5 – interest yield 14.63% – redemption yield 6.62%.

Therefore, with the price at 102.5, it might have appeared a good bargain to buy a 15% stock. However, the stock was dated 1997, and only had a few months to go before redemption – in fact, there was only one more half yearly interest payment due. This meant also that in a few months' time, the stock for which you had paid 102.5 would be redeemed at par – i.e. at 100.

In fact, as you would expect, the redemption yields of stocks with similar life spans are very similar, even though the interest yield may be quite different.

National Savings

National Savings is also a government department, and once again when you invest in National Savings, you are lending money to the government. National Savings have several different products. These are:

* National Savings Bank Investment Accounts.
* National Savings Certificates.
* Premium Bonds.
* National Savings Income Bonds.
* National Savings Capital Bonds.
* National Savings Pensioners Guaranteed Income Bonds.
* National Savings Fixed Rate Savings Bonds.
* National Savings Children's Bonus Bonds.

Each of these have different features.

National Savings Bank

This is, as the name implies, a savings bank which operates through all post offices. The only account available is the *National Savings Bank Investment Account*. This is a savings account which requires one month's notice for withdrawals. It gives higher rates of interest. There is a minimum investment of £20, and a maximum of £100,000. Higher rates of interest are paid on balances over £500. The interest is variable, paid gross, but is liable to tax.

National Savings Certificates

There are fixed Interest certificates and index linked certificates.

Fixed Interest Certificates

These are certificates issued by the National Savings office. You buy certificates in any amount from £100 to £15,000.

The interest is guaranteed for the five year term of the certificate. The interest is also free of tax. However, you may not draw on the interest before the five year term is finished. If you do need to cash in the certificates before the five year term, the interest rate is lower for the earlier years. If you do not cash in the certificates at the end of the five year term, they continue to earn interest, but only at a variable rate called the 'General Extension Rate'. This is lower than the normal rate on certificates.

Index Linked Certificates

These certificates are also issued for five year terms, and again you may invest from £100 to £15,000. The value at the end of the five year term is calculated in two parts.

One part is the index linked part. This means that the certificate's value increases by the increase in the retail prices index over the five year period.

The other part is the interest. Interest is given at a lower rate than the fixed interest certificates, and added to the value at the end of the five year term.

If you need to cash in early, the index linking applies after the first anniversary of the purchase, and interest is also added from that date, but at a lower rate. If you do not cash in the certificates at the end of the five year term, they continue to earn index linked 'extension terms', which are lower than the current rate on new issues.

Premium Bonds

You may invest a minimum of £100 to a maximum of £30,000 in Premium Bonds. They do not pay interest, but once you have held the Bonds for a full calendar month, your number goes into the prize draw.

There is one prize of £1 million every month, and a number of other prizes from £50 to £100,000. Each £1 unit has a fixed chance of 19,000 to 1 of winning a prize every month. The size of the prize fund determines how many prizes of each denomination there are (except the 'jackpot' prize of £1 million, one of which is guaranteed every month). The prize fund is determined by a notional rate of interest on the total value of Premium Bonds in issue.

The Bonds may be cashed in at any time without notice, at the same value for which they were purchased. The prizes are exempt from tax.

National Savings Income Bonds

You may invest a minimum of £500 up to a maximum of £1,000,000 in Income Bonds. They pay monthly interest at a variable rate, and the interest is paid gross – i.e. without deduction of income tax. The interest is taxable. The interest rate is fairly competitive, and a higher rate of interest applies for investments of £25,000 or more. Three months' notice is required for withdrawal, although you may cash them in without notice, but with a penalty equivalent to 90 days' interest.

National Savings Capital Bonds

You may invest a minimum of £100 up to a maximum of £1,000,000 in Capital Bonds. This is a lump sum investment with a fixed term of five years, and a fixed, guaranteed interest rate for the whole five year term. However, the interest rate is 'tiered'. This means that the interest starts at a lower figure for the first year, then increases each year to make up the full guaranteed amount at the end of the five year term.

The interest is not paid to you, but added to the amount of the Bond. National Savings send you a statement every year to show how the Bond has grown with the added interest. The interest is added gross, and the amount of the interest is taxable. You may cash in the Bond at any time without notice. Repayment is then made of the amount standing to your credit at the previous anniversary of the purchase, plus interest from then at the rate of interest for the last year. Thus, early cashing in means that you lose out on the full interest rate.

National Savings Pensioners Guaranteed Income Bonds

You must be over 60 years of age to buy these Bonds. You may invest a minimum of £500, up to a maximum of £1,000,000 in these Bonds. There are five-year bonds and two-year bonds.

The interest is at a guaranteed fixed rate for the term. Interest is paid monthly, and is paid gross. However, it is taxable.

You may cash in these Bonds early, but at 60 days' notice, and during the notice period, no interest is paid. Alternatively, you may cash them in without notice, but subject to a penalty of 90 days' interest on the amount withdrawn.

National Savings Fixed Rate Savings Bonds

You may invest a minimum of £500 and a maximum of £1,000,000 in these Bonds. Interest is paid monthly or annually, at a guaranteed rate for a period, but with tax deducted at source.

These Bonds are offered with four different fixed terms, of six months, one year, 18 months, or three years. The rate of interest depends on the term you choose, and the rate is tiered, with different rates for investments from £500 up to £20,000, from £20,000 up to £50,000, and over £50,000.

The Bonds are held for their full term, then National Savings will tell you what your options are at the completion of the term.

National Savings Children's Bonus Bonds

These may be opened by anyone over the age of 15, for anyone under that age. The minimum investment is £25, and the maximum £3,000. These figures are for each person on whose behalf the investment is made. Thus, a parent may put in up to £3,000 for each of their children, or any other children. The bonds are controlled by the child's parent or legal guardian, irrespective of who made the actual investment of money.

Interest is at a fixed, guaranteed rate for five years. At the end of the five year term, a bonus is added to the investment. This bonus is also fixed and guaranteed at the outset. The interest and the bonus are exempt from income tax.

When interest rates are changed, a new issue of these bonds is made. At that point, a new investment may be made in the new issue on top of what has already been invested.

These bonds may be cashed in early without notice, but again there is a loss of interest. Repayment will be made of the amount of the bond at the previous anniversary, plus interest at a daily rate up to the time of cashing in. Bonuses are not paid until the full five year term is finished. The bond may also be cashed in on the child's 21st birthday.

When you are in retirement, these can be useful for giving to grandchildren.

Appendix 5
Investing in Life Assurance Policies

Using Life Assurance as an investment

Whole Life Policies

Life Assurance in its simplest and purest form is a form of protection. You pay a regular premium, each month or each year, and when you die, your dependants get a lump sum which will be of help to them. There has to be an 'insurable interest'. This means that you cannot just take out a life assurance policy on somebody unconnected to you – say, the President of the United States – and then collect a lump sum when he dies. It has to be somebody whose death would otherwise cause you loss. This is most commonly a family member, but it can be a key person in your business whose death would cause a financial loss.

This type of policy is known as a 'whole life' policy. Cover is provided throughout the life of the person insured, provided the premiums are paid. It can also cover the lives of two people, usually husband and wife. It is then known as a 'joint life' policy.

Term Policies

Life assurance policies can be indefinite, or for a fixed term. A Term Policy would be taken out because the protection is only needed for a certain length of time – for example, during the period of repaying a mortgage.

A Level Term Policy is one in which the amount of the cover stays the same for the whole term of the policy. A Decreasing Term Policy is one in which the cover decreases year by year. This type of policy is often used in conjunction with repayment mortgages, where the balance on the mortgage account decreases each year, and the policy provides cover which broadly matches the decreasing balance.

Endowment Policies

However, a development of the simple 'protection' type policy was the Endowment Policy. This added on to the protection element, a savings element. The premiums are of course higher for this sort of policy. But the key feature is that they cover a definite period (the term), during which your life would be insured for a certain sum, but at the end of the term, (known as the maturity), if you are still alive, you receive a lump sum. The most common type of Endowment Policy is a 'with profits' policy. This means that the amount paid in each year is invested by the insurance company, and part of the profits each year are added to the value of the policy which is paid out at maturity.

This is done by the insurance company declaring 'reversionary bonuses' each year which are added to the value of the policy. These bonuses cannot be deducted once they have been added. Reversionary bonuses do not tend to suffer the extremes of fluctuations that other 'unit linked' policies do. This is because the bonuses are subject to a 'rolling average' adjustment. This ensures that large fluctuations in the value of the underlying investments are smoothed out, and a more level bonus is added each year. Then, at the maturity, a 'terminal bonus' is added. The terminal bonus is not guaranteed. The terminal bonus tends to fluctuate more than the reversionary bonus, because it is more affected by the actual increase or decrease in the value of the underlying investments of the particular year in which the terminal bonus is added.

Unitised Policies

Some Endowment Policies are unitised. That means that the premiums buy units in the with profits fund. The unit prices increase as the annual bonus is added on a daily basis. At the maturity of the policy, the value of the units plus a terminal bonus is paid out.

Bonds

Another relatively recent development has been the 'Insurance Bond'. This is in effect a single premium Endowment Assurance Policy, if it has a fixed term. If it continues until death, then it is an open ended whole of life policy. The fixed term is often five or ten years.

- **Income Bonds**. In return for a single premium paid 'up front' you receive a fixed income each year, and the return of the premium, sometimes with some increase added, at the end of the term. Because of tax regulations, these can be advantageous in certain cases.

- **Capital Growth Bonds**. The single premium is paid 'up front', but instead of the income being paid out, it 'rolls up' in the policy to provide a larger sum on maturity.

Commission

As with all insurance policies, if they are sold to you by tied agents or independent advisers, they may be subject to commission being paid. The effect of this is particularly noticeable with Bonds. The effect of the initial commission may be that if you wanted to withdraw the money in the early years, you might suffer a loss. Always check this before you invest.

Trading Endowment Policies

If you found that you could not keep up the premiums on Endowment Policies, in the past, the only thing to do was to surrender them to the insurance company. You could get back a certain amount, depending on the number of years you had been paying the premiums. However, the amount would always be at a large discount to the true value of your fund.

In recent years, a market has grown up in traded Endowment Policies. This means that instead of simply surrendering your Endowment Policy to the insurance company, you could sell them to another person who would continue to pay the premiums, and then collect the funds at maturity. In general, this method produces a larger amount than surrendering the policy.

Buying Traded Endowment Policies (TEPs) has also been seen as an investment tool. A person buying such a policy takes over the liability for the remaining premiums, and the policy continues on the life of the original person who sold the policy. The amount paid for the policy depends on several factors, of which the most obvious is the remaining time left until maturity. The earlier death of the original life assured would of course mean an earlier maturity.

This type of investment is fairly complex, and needs the advice of the market makers, of whom there are several specialising in this area. However, it is a relatively low risk investment, since the minimum value of the policy usually corresponds very closely to the purchase price and premiums paid. Then at maturity there is a relatively large amount added as terminal bonus.

Once again, however, the amount of the final benefit is at the mercy of the bonuses. In recent years, annual bonuses have fallen. In some cases, the terminal bonus is also lower, and the overall return for a purchased endowment policy could be disappointing.

Glossary of Terms

Actuarial valuation   Valuation of the fund of the pension scheme to assess whether it can meet its obligations.

Additional Voluntary Contribution   Extra contribution to an employer's pension scheme.

Annuity   The annual amount of pension payment.

Annuity rate   The rate at which a pension fund converts into an annuity.

Charging structure   The way in which the pension provider makes their charges for the pension scheme.

Concurrency   Having different pension schemes at the same time.

Contracting out   Paying additional pension contributions to a private scheme instead of the state second pension.

Deferral   Putting off the date of receiving the pension benefits.

Defined Benefit Scheme   An employer's scheme under which the pension benefit is related to the final salary.

Defined Contribution Scheme
An employer's scheme under which the pension benefit is related to the amount of the accumulated fund.

Executive Pension Plan
A specialised employer's pension scheme for directors or other executives.

Final Salary Scheme
See defined benefit scheme.

Group Personal Pensions
A form of personal pension plan for a group of people, usually sponsored by an employer.

Income drawdown
A way to receive the pension benefits from a personal pension plan without committing to an annuity.

Indexation
Annual increase in pension in line with inflation or a fixed percentage.

ISA
Tax exempt form of saving and investing.

Minimum Income Guarantee
Government policy underpinning the Pension Credit.

Money Purchase scheme
See defined contribution scheme.

Non-contributory scheme
Employer's pension scheme under which the employee does not make any contribution.

Open market option   The right to take the fund of a personal pension plan and use it to obtain pension benefits from another provider.

Permitted investments   Investments which are authorised under the scheme's trust document, or government restrictions.

Personal Pension Plan   Approved form of pension scheme with tax benefits.

Phased retirement   Taking retirement over a period of years, gradually increasing the pension benefits each year.

Prohibited investments   Investments which are not permitted under the scheme's trust document, or government restrictions.

Qualifying earnings   Earnings which entitle a person to make contributions to a personal pension plan.

Retirement Annuity Policy   Approved form of pension provision with tax benefits – now closed for new members, but still running for existing members.

Retirement benefits   The benefits under a pension scheme which apply when the member ceases work.

SERPS   A form of State Pension based on earnings-related contributions

SIPP Self Invested Personal Pension – under which the member has rights to decide the investments of the fund.

SSAS Small Self Administered Scheme – an employer's pension scheme which allows the trustees to make their choice of investments.

Stakeholder Pension A type of approved pension scheme with tax benefits.

Tax free lump sum The right to receive a tax free sum on retirement.

Top hat scheme *See executive pension plan.*

Additional reading and useful web sites

Additional reading

Books

Managing your money in retirement, John Whiteley (How To Books)

Going for self employment, John Whiteley (How To Books)

Small Business Tax Guide, John Whiteley (How To Books)

The Pensions Factbook, (Gee Publishing)

Tolley's Pension Handbook, (Tolleys)

Periodicals
(particularly useful for those administering pension funds)

Pensions Management

Pensions Week

Pensions World

Web sites:
www.find.co.uk A financial directory giving links to various providers of pensions and other financial products and services.

www.moneyweb.co.uk A financial information web site

186

giving general information and links to financial products and services.

www.sharingpensions.co.uk A web site giving information about pensions generally, but with commercial sponsorship.

www.moneyextra.com A web site giving general financial information.

www.opas.org.uk An independent web site giving much information and unbiassed advice about pensions.

www.dwp.gov.uk This is the web site of the Department of Work and Pensions, the government department dealing with benefits of all sorts – both in retirement and before retirement.

www.thepensionservice.gov.uk This is the government web site devoted to giving information about State Pensions.

www.fsa.gov.uk This is the web site of the Financial Services Authority, the regulatory body for all types of financial services, including financial and pension advisers.

www.opra.gov.uk This is the government web site for the Office of the Pensions Regulatory Authority, which has overall control and regulation of all pension schemes. It is the place to go for any queries about setting up a pension scheme.

Index

If you want to know how … to turn your business around

'This book has been written to act as a *fire extinguisher* for use in a crisis and a *smoke detector* to help spot the early warning signs of approaching difficulty while there is still time to do something about it.

'If you are in difficulty the first things to realise are: you are not alone; there are specific skills and techniques that can be used to avoid failure and; other people have been through this and survived – there are ways out, particularly with help!'

Mark Blayney

Turning Your Business Around
How to spot the warning signs and ensure a business stays healthy

Mark Blayney

'Inspiring and full of proven steps to help you trade out of tough times.' – *HSBC Business Update*

'A cheap and effective way of preparing proprietors of troubled businesses for the task ahead.' – *Recovery*

'Owners, managers and directors of small businesses will find this book, with its wealth of common sense principles, extremely helpful. And should you run into trouble, Mark Blayney offers sound advice.' – *Small Business Service*

ISBN 1 84528 063 6

If you want to know how ... to beat the pension crisis

'The aim of this book is simple: to help ensure that when you retire you have sufficient resources to afford a reasonable retirement.

'Perhaps the most striking feature of the not-so-brave new world of pensions is that we all need to build up our financial judgements. You can buy advice, which some people prefer; but even then you may fare better if you have some knowledge, both to ask the right questions and understand the answers. Talk to your friends, read newspapers – buy books like this!'

Anthony Vice

7 Ways to Beat the Pension Crisis

Anthony Vice

Since the year 2000, falling stock markets, failing final salary schemes, later retirement dates and lower annuity rates have all affected pensions, and by 2006 the Government will have substantially changed the rules under which pensions operate. Also people are living longer, and therefore costing the state and private pension schemes more at the very time when they are underfunded and underperforming. In this book Anthony Vice explains clearly the new 2005 rules and outlines *seven effective ways* in which you can secure a more prosperous retirement.

ISBN 1 85703 942 4

If you want to know how … to master small business finance

'Small businesses often find more difficulty than large businesses in managing their resources, and finance is one of the most important resources. The key to management of any resource is the ability to take control of it. The key to financial control is accurate measurement. In order to measure things accurately, certain techniques must be learnt. Those techniques form the bulk of this book.'

John Whiteley

Watching the Bottom Line
How to master the essential techniques for managing small business finances

John Whiteley

This book will show you exactly what's going on in your business and enable you to measure accurately its achievements.

There's also advice on:
- Getting the best from your bank
- Raising long term loan capital and short term finance
- Tax planning and compliance
- Rewarding employees
- Attracting investment
- Issuing shares
- Paying dividends
- How to get the best from leasing and hire purchase

ISBN 1 85703 989 0

How To Books are available through all good bookshops, or you can order direct from us through Grantham Book Services.

Tel: +44 (0)1476 541080
Fax: +44 (0)1476 541061
Email: orders@gbs.tbs-ltd.co.uk

Or via our website

www.howtobooks.co.uk

To order via any of these methods please quote the title(s) of the book(s) and your credit card number together with its expiry date.

For further information about our books and catalogue, please contact:

How To Books
3 Newtec Place
Magdalen Road
Oxford OX4 1RE

Visit our website at

www.howtobooks.co.uk

Or you can contact us by email at info@howtobooks.co.uk